Contents

Introduction

The International English Language Testing System (IELTS) is widely recognised as a reliable means of assessing the language ability of candidates who need to study or work where English is the language of communication. These Practice Tests are designed to give future IELTS candidates an idea of whether their English is at the required level.

IELTS is owned by three partners, the University of Cambridge ESOL Examinations, the British Council and IDP Education Pty Limited (through its subsidiary company, IELTS Australia Pty Limited). Further information on IELTS can be found on the IELTS website (www.ielts.org).

WHAT IS THE TEST FORMAT?

IELTS consists of six components. All candidates take the same Listening and Speaking tests. There is a choice of Reading and Writing tests according to whether a candidate is taking the Academic or General Training module.

Academic	General Training
For candidates taking the test for entry to undergraduate or postgraduate studies or for professional reasons.	For candidates taking the test for entry to vocational or training programmes not at degree level, for admission to secondary schools and for immigration purposes.

The test components are taken in the following order:

Listening 4 sections, 40 items approximately 30 minutes		
Academic Reading 3 sections, 40 items 60 minutes	OR	**General Training Reading** 3 sections, 40 items 60 minutes
Academic Writing 2 tasks 60 minutes	OR	**General Training Writing** 2 tasks 60 minutes
Speaking 11 to 14 minutes		
Total Test Time 2 hours 44 minutes		

Listening

This test consists of four sections, each with ten questions. The first two sections are concerned with social needs. The first section is a conversation between two speakers and the second section is a monologue. The final two sections are concerned with situations related to educational or training contexts. The third section is a conversation between up to four people and the fourth section is a monologue.

A variety of question types is used, including: multiple choice, short-answer questions, sentence completion, notes/form/table/summary/flow-chart completion, labelling a diagram/plan/map, classification, matching.

Candidates hear the recording once only and answer the questions as they listen. Ten minutes are allowed at the end for candidates to transfer their answers to the answer sheet.

Academic Reading

This test consists of three sections with 40 questions. There are three texts, which are taken from journals, books, magazines, and newspapers. The texts are on topics of general interest. At least one text contains detailed logical argument.

A variety of question types is used, including: multiple choice, short-answer questions, sentence completion, notes/summary/flow-chart/table completion, diagram label completion, classification, matching, choosing suitable paragraph headings from a list, identification of writer's views/claims – *yes, no, not given*, identification of information in the text – *true, false, not given*.

General Training Reading

This test consists of three sections with 40 questions. The texts are taken from notices, advertisements, leaflets, newspapers, instruction manuals, books and magazines. The first section contains texts relevant to basic linguistic survival in English, with tasks mainly concerned with providing factual information. The second section focuses on the work context and involves texts of more complex language. The third section involves reading more extended texts, with a more complex structure, but with the emphasis on descriptive and instructive rather than argumentative texts.

A variety of question types is used, including: multiple choice, short-answer questions, sentence completion, notes/summary/flow-chart/table completion, diagram label completion, classification, matching, choosing suitable paragraph headings from a list, identification of writer's views/claims – *yes, no, not given*, identification of information in the text – *true, false, not given*.

Academic Writing

This test consists of two tasks. It is suggested that candidates spend about 20 minutes on Task 1, which requires them to write at least 150 words, and 40 minutes on Task 2, which requires them to write at least 250 words. Task 2 contributes twice as much as Task 1 to the Writing score.

Task 1 requires candidates to look at a diagram or some data (graph, table or chart) and to present the information in their own words. They are assessed on their ability to organise, present and possibly compare data, describe the stages of a process, describe an object or event, or explain how something works.

In Task 2 candidates are presented with a point of view, argument or problem. They are assessed on their ability to present a solution to the problem, present and justify an opinion, compare and contrast evidence and opinions, and evaluate and challenge ideas, evidence or arguments.

Candidates are also assessed on their ability to write in an appropriate style.

General Training Writing

This test consists of two tasks. It is suggested that candidates spend about 20 minutes on Task 1, which requires them to write at least 150 words, and 40 minutes on Task 2, which requires them to write at least 250 words. Task 2 contributes twice as much as Task 1 to the Writing score.

In Task 1 candidates are asked to respond to a given situation with a letter requesting information or explaining the situation. They are assessed on their ability to engage in personal correspondence, elicit and provide general factual information, express needs, wants, likes and dislikes, express opinions, complaints, etc.

In Task 2 candidates are presented with a point of view, argument or problem. They are assessed on their ability to provide general factual information, outline a problem and present a solution, present and justify an opinion, and evaluate and challenge ideas, evidence or arguments.

Candidates are also assessed on their ability to write in an appropriate style. More information on assessing both the Academic and General Training Writing tests, including Writing Band Descriptors (public version), is available on the IELTS website.

Speaking

This test takes between 11 and 14 minutes and is conducted by a trained examiner. There are three parts:

Part 1
The candidate and the examiner introduce themselves. Candidates then answer general questions about themselves, their home/family, their job/studies, their interests and a wide range of similar familiar topic areas. This part lasts between four and five minutes.

Part 2
The candidate is given a task card with prompts and is asked to talk on a particular topic. The candidate has one minute to prepare and they can make some notes if they wish, before speaking for between one and two minutes. The examiner then asks one or two rounding-off questions.

Part 3
The examiner and the candidate engage in a discussion of more abstract issues which are thematically linked to the topic in Part 2. The discussion lasts between four and five minutes.

The Speaking test assesses whether candidates can communicate effectively in English. The assessment takes into account Fluency and Coherence, Lexical Resource, Grammatical

Range and Accuracy, and Pronunciation. More information on assessing the Speaking test, including Speaking Band Descriptors (public version), is available on the IELTS website.

HOW IS IELTS SCORED?

IELTS results are reported on a nine-band scale. In addition to the score for overall language ability, IELTS provides a score in the form of a profile for each of the four skills (Listening, Reading, Writing and Speaking). These scores are also reported on a nine-band scale. All scores are recorded on the Test Report Form along with details of the candidate's nationality, first language and date of birth. Each Overall Band Score corresponds to a descriptive statement which gives a summary of the English language ability of a candidate classified at that level. The nine bands and their descriptive statements are as follows:

9 **Expert User** – *Has fully operational command of the language: appropriate, accurate and fluent with complete understanding.*

8 **Very Good User** – *Has fully operational command of the language with only occasional unsystematic inaccuracies and inappropriacies. Misunderstandings may occur in unfamiliar situations. Handles complex detailed argumentation well.*

7 **Good User** – *Has operational command of the language, though with occasional inaccuracies, inappropriacies and misunderstandings in some situations. Generally handles complex language well and understands detailed reasoning.*

6 **Competent User** – *Has generally effective command of the language despite some inaccuracies, inappropriacies and misunderstandings. Can use and understand fairly complex language, particularly in familiar situations.*

5 **Modest User** – *Has partial command of the language, coping with overall meaning in most situations, though is likely to make many mistakes. Should be able to handle basic communication in own field.*

4 **Limited User** – *Basic competence is limited to familiar situations. Has frequent problems in understanding and expression. Is not able to use complex language.*

3 **Extremely Limited User** – *Conveys and understands only general meaning in very familiar situations. Frequent breakdowns in communication occur.*

2 **Intermittent User** – *No real communication is possible except for the most basic information using isolated words or short formulae in familiar situations and to meet immediate needs. Has great difficulty understanding spoken and written English.*

1 **Non User** – *Essentially has no ability to use the language beyond possibly a few isolated words.*

0 **Did not attempt the test** – *No assessable information provided.*

Most universities and colleges in the United Kingdom, Australia, New Zealand, Canada and the USA accept an IELTS Overall Band Score of 6.0 – 7.0 for entry to academic programmes.

MARKING THE PRACTICE TESTS

Listening and Reading

The Answer keys are on pages 152–161.
Each question in the Listening and Reading tests is worth one mark.

Questions which require letter/Roman numeral answers
- For questions where the answers are letters or Roman numerals, you should write *only* the number of answers required. For example, if the answer is a single letter or numeral you should write only one answer. If you have written more letters or numerals than are required, the answer must be marked wrong.

Questions which require answers in the form of words or numbers
- Answers may be written in upper or lower case.
- Words in brackets are optional – they are correct, but not necessary.
- Alternative answers are separated by a slash (/).
- If you are asked to write an answer using a certain number of words and/or (a) number(s), you will be penalised if you exceed this. For example, if a question specifies an answer using NO MORE THAN THREE WORDS and the correct answer is 'black leather coat', the answer 'coat of black leather' is incorrect.
- In questions where you are expected to complete a gap, you should transfer only the necessary missing word(s) onto the answer sheet. For example, to complete 'in the …', and the correct answer is 'morning', the answer 'in the morning' would be incorrect.
- All answers require correct spelling (including words in brackets).
- Both US and UK spelling are acceptable and are included in the Answer key.
- All standard alternatives for numbers, dates and currencies are acceptable.
- All standard abbreviations are acceptable.
- You will find additional notes about individual answers in the Answer key.

Writing

The model and sample answers are on pages 162–173. It is not possible for you to give yourself a mark for the Writing tasks. For Task 2 in Tests 1 and 3, and Task 1 in Tests 2 and 4, and for Task 1 in General Training Test A and Task 2 in General Training Test B, we have provided model answers (written by an examiner). It is important to note that these show just one way of completing the task, out of many possible approaches. For Task 1 in Tests 1 and 3, and Task 2 in Tests 2 and 4, and for Task 2 in General Training Test A and Task 1 in General Training Test B, we have provided sample answers (written by candidates), showing their score and the examiner's comments. These model answers and sample answers will give you an insight into what is required for the Writing test.

HOW SHOULD YOU INTERPRET YOUR SCORES?

At the end of each Listening and Reading Answer key you will find a chart which will help you assess whether, on the basis of your Practice Test results, you are ready to take the IELTS test.

In interpreting your score, there are a number of points you should bear in mind. Your performance in the real IELTS test will be reported in two ways: there will be a Band Score from 1 to 9 for each of the components and an Overall Band Score from 1 to 9, which is the average of your scores in the four components. However, institutions considering your application are advised to look at both the Overall Band Score and the Bands for each component in order to determine whether you have the language skills needed for a particular course of study. For example, if your course has a lot of reading and writing, but no lectures, listening skills might be less important and a score of 5 in Listening might be acceptable if the Overall Band Score was 7. However, for a course which has lots of lectures and spoken instructions, a score of 5 in Listening might be unacceptable even though the Overall Band Score was 7.

Once you have marked your tests you should have some idea of whether your listening and reading skills are good enough for you to try the IELTS test. If you did well enough in one component but not in others, you will have to decide for yourself whether you are ready to take the test.

The Practice Tests have been checked to ensure that they are of approximately the same level of difficulty as the real IELTS test. However, we cannot guarantee that your score in the Practice Tests will be reflected in the real IELTS test. The Practice Tests can only give you an idea of your possible future performance and it is ultimately up to you to make decisions based on your score.

Different institutions accept different IELTS scores for different types of courses. We have based our recommendations on the average scores which the majority of institutions accept. The institution to which you are applying may, of course, require a higher or lower score than most other institutions.

Further information

For more information about IELTS or any other University of Cambridge ESOL examination, write to:

University of Cambridge ESOL Examinations
1 Hills Road
Cambridge
CB1 2EU
United Kingdom

Telephone: +44 1223 553355
Fax: +44 1223 460278
email: esolhelpdesk@cambridgeesol.org
http://www.cambridgeesol.org
http://www.ielts.org

Test 1

SECTION 1   *Questions 1–10*

Questions 1–5

Complete the notes below.

*Write **NO MORE THAN THREE WORDS** for each answer.*

Transport from Airport to Milton

Example	*Answer*
Distance:	.......*147*........ miles

Options:

• Car hire
   – don't want to drive

• **1** ....
   – expensive

• Greyhound bus
   – $15 single, $27.50 return
   – direct to the **2** ....
   – long **3** ....

• Airport Shuttle
   – **4** .... service
   – every 2 hours
   – $35 single, $65 return
   – need to **5** ....

10

Questions 6–10

Complete the booking form below.

*Write **ONE WORD AND/OR A NUMBER** for each answer.*

AIRPORT SHUTTLE BOOKING FORM

To: Milton

Date: 6 ....   **No. of passengers:**   One

Bus Time: 7 .... pm   **Type of ticket:**   Single

Name: Janet 8 ....

Flight No: 9 ....   **From:**   London Heathrow

Address in Milton: Vacation Motel,
24, Kitchener Street

Fare: $35
Credit Card No: (Visa) 10 ....

SECTION 2　　*Questions 11–20*

Questions 11–16

*Choose the correct letter, **A**, **B** or **C**.*

11　PS Camping has been organising holidays for

　　A　15 years.
　　B　20 years.
　　C　25 years.

12　The company has most camping sites in

　　A　France.
　　B　Italy.
　　C　Switzerland.

13　Which organised activity can children do every day of the week?

　　A　football
　　B　drama
　　C　model making

14　Some areas of the sites have a 'no noise' rule after

　　A　9.30 p.m.
　　B　10.00 p.m.
　　C　10.30 p.m.

15　The holiday insurance that is offered by PS Camping

　　A　can be charged on an annual basis.
　　B　is included in the price of the holiday.
　　C　must be taken out at the time of booking.

16　Customers who recommend PS Camping to friends will receive

　　A　a free gift.
　　B　an upgrade to a luxury tent.
　　C　a discount.

Questions 17–20

What does the speaker say about the following items?

Write the correct letter, A, B or C, next to questions 17–20.

A	They are provided in all tents.
B	They are found in central areas of the campsite.
C	They are available on request.

17 barbecues   ....

18 toys   ....

19 cool boxes   ....

20 mops and buckets   ....

SECTION 3   *Questions 21–30*

Questions 21–23

Complete the notes below.

*Write **ONE WORD ONLY** for each answer.*

DIFFERENCES BETWEEN INDIVIDUALS IN THE WORKPLACE

Individuals bring different:

- ideas
- **21** ....
- learning experiences

Work behaviour differences are due to:

- personality
- **22** ....

Effects of diversity on companies:

Advantage: diversity develops **23** ....
Disadvantage: diversity can cause conflict

Questions 24–27

*Choose the correct letter, **A**, **B** or **C**.*

24 Janice thinks that employers should encourage workers who are

   A   potential leaders.
   B   open to new ideas.
   C   good at teamwork.

25 Janice suggests that managers may find it difficult to

   A   form successful groups.
   B   balance conflicting needs.
   C   deal with uncooperative workers.

26 Janice believes employers should look for job applicants who

   A   can think independently.
   B   will obey the system.
   C   can solve problems.

27 Janice believes managers should

   A   demonstrate good behaviour.
   B   encourage co-operation early on.
   C   increase financial incentives.

Questions 28–30

Complete the sentences below.

*Write **ONE WORD ONLY** for each answer.*

28 All managers need to understand their employees and recognise their company's
   ....

29 When managing change, increasing the company's .... may be more
   important than employee satisfaction.

30 During periods of change, managers may have to cope with increased amounts of
   ....

SECTION 4   *Questions 31–40*

Questions 31–35

Complete the notes below.

Write ONE WORD ONLY for each answer.

SEMINAR ON ROCK ART

Preparation for fieldwork trip to Namibia in **31** ....

Rock art in Namibia may be

• paintings
• engravings

Earliest explanation of engravings of animal footprints

They were used to help **32** .... learn about tracking

But:

• Why are the tracks usually **33** .... ?
• Why are some engravings realistic and others unrealistic?
• Why are the unrealistic animals sometimes half **34** .... ?

More recent explanation:

Wise men may have been trying to control wild animals with **35** ....

Comment:

Earlier explanation was due to scholars over-generalising from their experience of a different culture.

Questions 36–40

Complete the sentences below.

*Write **ONE WORD ONLY** for each answer.*

36   If you look at a site from a .... , you reduce visitor pressure.

37   To camp on a site may be disrespectful to people from that ....

38   Undiscovered material may be damaged by ....

39   You should avoid .... or tracing rock art as it is so fragile.

40   In general, your aim is to leave the site ....

READING

READING PASSAGE 1

*You should spend about 20 minutes on **Questions 1–13**, which are based on Reading Passage 1 below.*

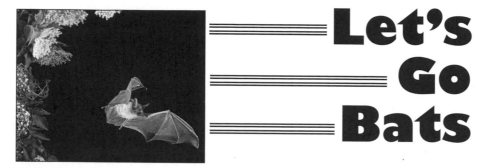

Let's Go Bats

A   Bats have a problem: how to find their way around in the dark. They hunt at night, and cannot use light to help them find prey and avoid obstacles. You might say that this is a problem of their own making, one that they could avoid simply by changing their habits and hunting by day. But the daytime economy is already heavily exploited by other creatures such as birds. Given that there is a living to be made at night, and given that alternative daytime trades are thoroughly occupied, natural selection has favoured bats that make a go of the night-hunting trade. It is probable that the nocturnal trades go way back in the ancestry of all mammals. In the time when the dinosaurs dominated the daytime economy, our mammalian ancestors probably only managed to survive at all because they found ways of scraping a living at night. Only after the mysterious mass extinction of the dinosaurs about 65 million years ago were our ancestors able to emerge into the daylight in any substantial numbers.

B   Bats have an engineering problem: how to find their way and find their prey in the absence of light. Bats are not the only creatures to face this difficulty today. Obviously the night-flying insects that they prey on must find their way about somehow. Deep-sea fish and whales have little or no light by day or by night. Fish and dolphins that live in extremely muddy water cannot see because, although there is light, it is obstructed and scattered by the dirt in the water. Plenty of other modern animals make their living in conditions where seeing is difficult or impossible.

C   Given the questions of how to manoeuvre in the dark, what solutions might an engineer consider? The first one that might occur to him is to manufacture light, to use a lantern or a searchlight. Fireflies and some fish (usually with the help of bacteria) have the power to manufacture their own light, but the process seems to consume a large amount of energy. Fireflies use their light for attracting mates. This doesn't require a prohibitive amount of energy: a male's tiny pinprick of light can be seen by a female from some distance on a dark night, since her eyes are exposed directly to the light source itself. However, using light to find one's own way around requires vastly more energy, since the eyes have to detect the tiny fraction of the light that bounces off each part of the scene. The light source must therefore be immensely brighter if it is to be used as a headlight to illuminate the path, than if it is to be used as a signal to others. In any event, whether or not the reason is the energy expense, it seems to be the case that, with the possible exception of some weird deep-sea fish, no animal apart from man uses manufactured light to find its way about.

D What else might the engineer think of? Well, blind humans sometimes seem to have an uncanny sense of obstacles in their path. It has been given the name 'facial vision', because blind people have reported that it feels a bit like the sense of touch, on the face. One report tells of a totally blind boy who could ride his tricycle at good speed round the block near his home, using facial vision. Experiments showed that, in fact, facial vision is nothing to do with touch or the front of the face, although the sensation may be referred to the front of the face, like the referred pain in a phantom limb. The sensation of facial vision, it turns out, really goes in through the ears. Blind people, without even being aware of the fact, are actually using echoes of their own footsteps and of other sounds, to sense the presence of obstacles. Before this was discovered, engineers had already built instruments to exploit the principle, for example to measure the depth of the sea under a ship. After this technique had been invented, it was only a matter of time before weapons designers adapted it for the detection of submarines. Both sides in the Second World War relied heavily on these devices, under such codenames as Asdic (British) and Sonar (American), as well as Radar (American) or RDF (British), which uses radio echoes rather than sound echoes.

E The Sonar and Radar pioneers didn't know it then, but all the world now knows that bats, or rather natural selection working on bats, had perfected the system tens of millions of years earlier, and their 'radar' achieves feats of detection and navigation that would strike an engineer dumb with admiration. It is technically incorrect to talk about bat 'radar', since they do not use radio waves. It is sonar. But the underlying mathematical theories of radar and sonar are very similar, and much of our scientific understanding of the details of what bats are doing has come from applying radar theory to them. The American zoologist Donald Griffin, who was largely responsible for the discovery of sonar in bats, coined the term 'echolocation' to cover both sonar and radar, whether used by animals or by human instruments.

Questions 1–5

Reading Passage 1 has five paragraphs, **A–E**.

Which paragraph contains the following information?

*Write the correct letter, **A–E**, in boxes 1–5 on your answer sheet.*

NB   *You may use any letter more than once.*

1   examples of wildlife other than bats which do not rely on vision to navigate by

2   how early mammals avoided dying out

3   why bats hunt in the dark

4   how a particular discovery has helped our understanding of bats

5   early military uses of echolocation

Questions 6–9

Complete the summary below.

*Choose **ONE WORD ONLY** from the passage for each answer.*

Write your answers in boxes 6–9 on your answer sheet.

Facial Vision

Blind people report that so-called 'facial vision' is comparable to the sensation of touch on the face. In fact, the sensation is more similar to the way in which pain from a **6** .... arm or leg might be felt. The ability actually comes from perceiving **7** .... through the ears. However, even before this was understood, the principle had been applied in the design of instruments which calculated the **8** .... of the seabed. This was followed by a wartime application in devices for finding **9** ....

Questions 10–13

Complete the sentences below.

*Choose **NO MORE THAN TWO WORDS** from the passage for each answer.*

Write your answers in boxes 10–13 on your answer sheet.

10   Long before the invention of radar, ... had resulted in a sophisticated radar-like system in bats.

11   Radar is an inaccurate term when referring to bats because .... are not used in their navigation system.

12   Radar and sonar are based on similar ....

13   The word 'echolocation' was first used by someone working as a ....

READING PASSAGE 2

*You should spend about 20 minutes on **Questions 14–26**, which are based on Reading Passage 2 on the following pages.*

Questions 14–20

Reading Passage 2 has seven paragraphs, **A–H**.

*Choose the correct heading for paragraphs **A** and **C–H** from the list of headings below.*

*Write the correct number, **i–xi**, in boxes 14–20 on your answer sheet.*

List of Headings

i	Scientists' call for a revision of policy
ii	An explanation for reduced water use
iii	How a global challenge was met
iv	Irrigation systems fall into disuse
v	Environmental effects
vi	The financial cost of recent technological improvements
vii	The relevance to health
viii	Addressing the concern over increasing populations
ix	A surprising downward trend in demand for water
x	The need to raise standards
xi	A description of ancient water supplies

---

14 Paragraph **A**

Example	*Answer*
Paragraph **B**	**iii**

---

15 Paragraph **C**

16 Paragraph **D**

17 Paragraph **E**

18 Paragraph **F**

19 Paragraph **G**

20 Paragraph **H**

MAKING EVERY DROP COUNT

A   The history of human civilisation is entwined with the history of the ways we have learned to manipulate water resources. As towns gradually expanded, water was brought from increasingly remote sources, leading to sophisticated engineering efforts such as dams and aqueducts. At the height of the Roman Empire, nine major systems, with an innovative layout of pipes and well-built sewers, supplied the occupants of Rome with as much water per person as is provided in many parts of the industrial world today.

B   During the industrial revolution and population explosion of the 19th and 20th centuries, the demand for water rose dramatically. Unprecedented construction of tens of thousands of monumental engineering projects designed to control floods, protect clean water supplies, and provide water for irrigation and hydropower brought great benefits to hundreds of millions of people. Food production has kept pace with soaring populations mainly because of the expansion of artificial irrigation systems that make possible the growth of 40 % of the world's food. Nearly one fifth of all the electricity generated worldwide is produced by turbines spun by the power of falling water.

C   Yet there is a dark side to this picture: despite our progress, half of the world's population still suffers, with water services inferior to those available to the ancient Greeks and Romans. As the United Nations report on access to water reiterated in November 2001, more than one billion people lack access to clean drinking water; some two and a half billion do not have adequate sanitation services. Preventable water-related diseases kill an estimated 10,000 to 20,000 children every day, and the latest evidence suggests that we are falling behind in efforts to solve these problems.

D   The consequences of our water policies extend beyond jeopardising human health. Tens of millions of people have been forced to move from their homes – often with little warning or compensation – to make way for the reservoirs behind dams. More than 20 % of all freshwater fish species are now threatened or endangered because dams and water withdrawals have destroyed the free-flowing river ecosystems where they thrive. Certain irrigation practices degrade soil quality and reduce agricultural productivity. Groundwater aquifers* are being pumped down faster than they are naturally replenished in parts of India, China, the USA and elsewhere. And disputes over shared water resources have led to violence and continue to raise local, national and even international tensions.

---

* underground stores of water

E   At the outset of the new millennium, however, the way resource planners think about water is beginning to change. The focus is slowly shifting back to the provision of basic human and environmental needs as top priority – ensuring 'some for all,' instead of 'more for some'. Some water experts are now demanding that existing infrastructure be used in smarter ways rather than building new facilities, which is increasingly considered the option of last, not first, resort. This shift in philosophy has not been universally accepted, and it comes with strong opposition from some established water organisations. Nevertheless, it may be the only way to address successfully the pressing problems of providing everyone with clean water to drink, adequate water to grow food and a life free from preventable water-related illness.

F   Fortunately – and unexpectedly – the demand for water is not rising as rapidly as some predicted. As a result, the pressure to build new water infrastructures has diminished over the past two decades. Although population, industrial output and economic productivity have continued to soar in developed nations, the rate at which people withdraw water from aquifers, rivers and lakes has slowed. And in a few parts of the world, demand has actually fallen.

G   What explains this remarkable turn of events? Two factors: people have figured out how to use water more efficiently, and communities are rethinking their priorities for water use. Throughout the first three-quarters of the 20th century, the quantity of freshwater consumed per person doubled on average; in the USA, water withdrawals increased tenfold while the population quadrupled. But since 1980, the amount of water consumed per person has actually decreased, thanks to a range of new technologies that help to conserve water in homes and industry. In 1965, for instance, Japan used approximately 13 million gallons* of water to produce $1 million of commercial output; by 1989 this had dropped to 3.5 million gallons (even accounting for inflation) – almost a quadrupling of water productivity. In the USA, water withdrawals have fallen by more than 20 % from their peak in 1980.

H   On the other hand, dams, aqueducts and other kinds of infrastructure will still have to be built, particularly in developing countries where basic human needs have not been met. But such projects must be built to higher specifications and with more accountability to local people and their environment than in the past. And even in regions where new projects seem warranted, we must find ways to meet demands with fewer resources, respecting ecological criteria and to a smaller budget.

---

* 1 gallon: 4.546 litres

Questions 21–26

Do the following statements agree with the information given in Reading Passage 2?

In boxes 21–26 on your answer sheet, write

YES	*if the statement agrees with the claims of the writer*
NO	*if the statement contradicts the claims of the writer*
NOT GIVEN	*if it is impossible to say what the writer thinks about this*

21   Water use per person is higher in the industrial world than it was in Ancient Rome.

22   Feeding increasing populations is possible due primarily to improved irrigation systems.

23   Modern water systems imitate those of the ancient Greeks and Romans.

24   Industrial growth is increasing the overall demand for water.

25   Modern technologies have led to a reduction in domestic water consumption.

26   In the future, governments should maintain ownership of water infrastructures.

READING PASSAGE 3

*You should spend about 20 minutes on **Questions 27–40**, which are based on Reading Passage 3 below.*

EDUCATING PSYCHE

Educating Psyche by Bernie Neville is a book which looks at radical new approaches to learning, describing the effects of emotion, imagination and the unconscious on learning. One theory discussed in the book is that proposed by George Lozanov, which focuses on the power of suggestion.

Lozanov's instructional technique is based on the evidence that the connections made in the brain through unconscious processing (which he calls non-specific mental reactivity) are more durable than those made through conscious processing. Besides the laboratory evidence for this, we know from our experience that we often remember what we have perceived peripherally, long after we have forgotten what we set out to learn. If we think of a book we studied months or years ago, we will find it easier to recall peripheral details – the colour, the binding, the typeface, the table at the library where we sat while studying it – than the content on which we were concentrating. If we think of a lecture we listened to with great concentration, we will recall the lecturer's appearance and mannerisms, our place in the auditorium, the failure of the air-conditioning, much more easily than the ideas we went to learn. Even if these peripheral details are a bit elusive, they come back readily in hypnosis or when we relive the event imaginatively, as in psychodrama. The details of the content of the lecture, on the other hand, seem to have gone forever.

This phenomenon can be partly attributed to the common counterproductive approach to study (making extreme efforts to memorise, tensing muscles, inducing fatigue), but it also simply reflects the way the brain functions. Lozanov therefore made indirect instruction (suggestion) central to his teaching system. In suggestopedia, as he called his method, consciousness is shifted away from the curriculum to focus on something peripheral. The curriculum then becomes peripheral and is dealt with by the reserve capacity of the brain.

The suggestopedic approach to foreign language learning provides a good illustration. In its most recent variant (1980), it consists of the reading of vocabulary and text while the class is listening to music. The first session is in two parts. In the first part, the music is classical (Mozart, Beethoven, Brahms) and the teacher reads the text slowly and solemnly, with attention to the dynamics of the music. The students follow the text in their books. This is followed by several minutes of silence. In the second part, they listen to baroque music (Bach, Corelli, Handel) while the teacher reads the text in a normal speaking voice. During this time they have their books closed. During the whole of this session, their attention is passive; they listen to the music but make no attempt to learn the material.

Beforehand, the students have been carefully prepared for the language learning experience. Through meeting with the staff and satisfied students they develop the expectation that learning will be easy and pleasant and that they will successfully learn several hundred words of the foreign language during the class. In a preliminary talk, the teacher introduces them to the material to be covered, but does not 'teach' it. Likewise, the students are instructed not to try to learn it during this introduction.

Some hours after the two-part session, there is a follow-up class at which the students are stimulated to recall the material presented. Once again the approach is indirect. The students do not focus their attention on trying to remember the vocabulary, but focus on using the language to communicate (e.g. through games or improvised dramatisations). Such methods are not unusual in language teaching. What is distinctive in the suggestopedic method is that they are devoted entirely to assisting recall. The 'learning' of the material is assumed to be automatic and effortless, accomplished while listening to music. The teacher's task is to assist the students to apply what they have learned paraconsciously, and in doing so to make it easily accessible to consciousness. Another difference from conventional teaching is the evidence that students can regularly learn 1000 new words of a foreign language during a suggestopedic session, as well as grammar and idiom.

Lozanov experimented with teaching by direct suggestion during sleep, hypnosis and trance states, but found such procedures unnecessary. Hypnosis, yoga, Silva mind-control, religious ceremonies and faith healing are all associated with successful suggestion, but none of their techniques seem to be essential to it. Such rituals may be seen as placebos. Lozanov acknowledges that the ritual surrounding suggestion in his own system is also a placebo, but maintains that without such a placebo people are unable or afraid to tap the reserve capacity of their brains. Like any placebo, it must be dispensed with authority to be effective. Just as a doctor calls on the full power of autocratic suggestion by insisting that the patient take precisely this white capsule precisely three times a day before meals, Lozanov is categoric in insisting that the suggestopedic session be conducted exactly in the manner designated, by trained and accredited suggestopedic teachers.

While suggestopedia has gained some notoriety through success in the teaching of modern languages, few teachers are able to emulate the spectacular results of Lozanov and his associates. We can, perhaps, attribute mediocre results to an inadequate placebo effect. The students have not developed the appropriate mind set. They are often not motivated to learn through this method. They do not have enough 'faith'. They do not see it as 'real teaching', especially as it does not seem to involve the 'work' they have learned to believe is essential to learning.

Questions 27–30

*Choose the correct letter, **A**, **B**, **C** or **D**.*

Write the correct letter in boxes 27–30 on your answer sheet.

27 The book *Educating Psyche* is mainly concerned with

    A   the power of suggestion in learning.
    B   a particular technique for learning based on emotions.
    C   the effects of emotion on the imagination and the unconscious.
    D   ways of learning which are not traditional.

28 Lozanov's theory claims that, when we try to remember things,

    A   unimportant details are the easiest to recall.
    B   concentrating hard produces the best results.
    C   the most significant facts are most easily recalled.
    D   peripheral vision is not important.

29 In this passage, the author uses the examples of a book and a lecture to illustrate that

    A   both of these are important for developing concentration.
    B   his theory about methods of learning is valid.
    C   reading is a better technique for learning than listening.
    D   we can remember things more easily under hypnosis.

30 Lozanov claims that teachers should train students to

    A   memorise details of the curriculum.
    B   develop their own sets of indirect instructions.
    C   think about something other than the curriculum content.
    D   avoid overloading the capacity of the brain.

Questions 31–36

Do the following statements agree with the information given in Reading Passage 3?

In boxes 31–36 on your answer sheet, write

> **TRUE**   *if the statement agrees with the information*
> **FALSE**   *if the statement contradicts the information*
> **NOT GIVEN**   *if there is no information on this*

31   In the example of suggestopedic teaching in the fourth paragraph, the only variable that changes is the music.

32   Prior to the suggestopedia class, students are made aware that the language experience will be demanding.

33   In the follow-up class, the teaching activities are similar to those used in conventional classes.

34   As an indirect benefit, students notice improvements in their memory.

35   Teachers say they prefer suggestopedia to traditional approaches to language teaching.

36   Students in a suggestopedia class retain more new vocabulary than those in ordinary classes.

Questions 37–40

*Complete the summary using the list of words, **A–K**, below.*

*Write the correct letter, **A–K**, in boxes 37–40 on your answer sheet.*

Suggestopedia uses a less direct method of suggestion than other techniques such as hypnosis. However, Lozanov admits that a certain amount of **37** .... is necessary in order to convince students, even if this is just a **38** .... Furthermore, if the method is to succeed, teachers must follow a set procedure. Although Lozanov's method has become quite **39** .... , the results of most other teachers using this method have been **40** ....

A spectacular	**B** teaching	**C** lesson
D authoritarian	**E** unpopular	**F** ritual
G unspectacular	**H** placebo	**I** involved
J appropriate	**K** well known	

WRITING

WRITING TASK 1

You should spend about 20 minutes on this task.

> *The table below gives information on consumer spending on different items in five different countries in 2002.*
>
> *Summarise the information by selecting and reporting the main features, and make comparisons where relevant.*

Write at least 150 words.

Percentage of national consumer expenditure by category – 2002

Country	Food/Drinks/Tobacco	Clothing/Footwear	Leisure/Education
Ireland	28.91%	6.43%	2.21%
Italy	16.36%	9.00%	3.20%
Spain	18.80%	6.51%	1.98%
Sweden	15.77%	5.40%	3.22%
Turkey	32.14%	6.63%	4.35%

WRITING TASK 2

You should spend about 40 minutes on this task.

Write about the following topic:

> *It is generally believed that some people are born with certain talents, for instance for sport or music, and others are not. However, it is sometimes claimed that any child can be taught to become a good sports person or musician.*
>
> *Discuss both these views and give your own opinion.*

Give reasons for your answer and include any relevant examples from your own knowledge or experience.

Write at least 250 words.

SPEAKING

PART 1

The examiner asks the candidate about him/herself, his/her home, work or studies and other familiar topics.

EXAMPLE

Keeping in contact with people

- How do you usually contact your friends? [Why?]
- Do you prefer to contact different people in different ways? [Why?]
- Do you find it easy to keep in contact with friends and family? [Why/Why not?]
- In your country, did people in the past keep in contact in the same ways as they do today? [Why/Why not?]

PART 2

Describe a party that you enjoyed.

You should say:
   whose party it was and what it was celebrating
   where the party was held and who went to it
   what people did during the party
and explain what you enjoyed about this party.

You will have to talk about the topic for one to two minutes.
You have one minute to think about what you are going to say.
You can make some notes to help you if you wish.

PART 3

Discussion topics:

Family parties

Example questions:
What are the main reasons why people organise family parties in your country?
In some places people spend a lot of money on parties that celebrate special family events. Is this ever true in your country? Do you think this is a good trend or a bad trend?
Are there many differences between family parties and parties given by friends? Why do you think this is?

National celebrations

Example questions:
What kinds of national celebration do you have in your country?
Who tends to enjoy national celebrations more: young people or old people? Why?
Why do you think some people think that national celebrations are a waste of government money? Would you agree or disagree with this view? Why?

Test 2

SECTION 1   *Questions 1–10*

Complete the form below.

*Write **NO MORE THAN THREE WORDS AND/OR A NUMBER** for each answer.*

CAR INSURANCE

Example	*Answer*
Name:	Patrick Jones

Address: 1 .... , *Greendale*
Contact number: *730453*
Occupation: 2 ....

Size of car engine: *1200cc*

Type of car:
    Manufacturer: *Hewton*
    Model: 3 ....
    Year: *1997*

Previous insurance company:

4 ....

Any insurance claims in the last five years?

Yes ☑
No ☐

If yes, give brief details:

Car was **5** .... *in 1999*

Name(s) of other driver(s):
Simon **6** ....
Relationship to main driver:
7 ....

Uses of car: – *social*
       – **8** ....

Start date: *31 January*

Recommended Insurance arrangement

Name of company: 9 ....
Annual cost: 10 $ ....

SECTION 2   *Questions 11–20*

Questions 11 and 12

Label the map below.

*Write **NO MORE THAN TWO WORDS** for each answer.*

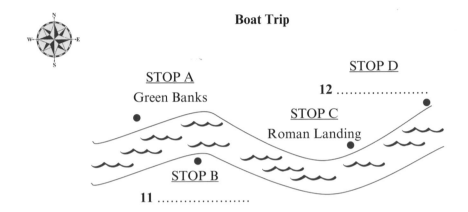

Boat Trip

STOP D

STOP A
Green Banks

12 ....

STOP C
Roman Landing

STOP B

11 ....

Questions 13–18

Complete the table below.

*Write **NO MORE THAN TWO WORDS AND/OR A NUMBER** for each answer.*

	Attraction	**Further Information**
STOP A: Main Booking Office: First boat: 8 a.m. Last boat: 13 .... p.m.	Palace	• has lovely **14** ....
STOP B:	**15**	• has good **16** .... of city centre
STOP C:	Museum	• bookshop specialising in the **17** .... of the local area
STOP D:	Entertainment Complex	• **18** .... cinema • bowling alley • video games arcade

Questions 19 and 20

*Write **NO MORE THAN THREE WORDS AND/OR A NUMBER** for each answer.*

19 How often do the Top Bus Company tours run?

....

20 Where can you catch a Number One Sightseeing Tour from?

....

SECTION 3   *Questions 21–30*

Questions 21–26

*Choose the correct letter, **A**, **B** or **C**.*

21 The Antarctic Centre was established in Christchurch because

    A   New Zealand is a member of the Antarctic Treaty.
    B   Christchurch is geographically well positioned.
    C   the climate of Christchurch is suitable.

22 One role of the Antarctic Centre is to

    A   provide expeditions with suitable equipment.
    B   provide researchers with financial assistance.
    C   ensure that research is internationally relevant.

23 The purpose of the Visitors' Centre is to

    A   provide accommodation.
    B   run training sessions.
    C   show people what Antarctica is like.

24 Dr Merrywhether says that Antarctica is

    A   unlike any other country.
    B   extremely beautiful.
    C   too cold for tourists.

25 According to Dr Merrywhether, Antarctica is very cold because

    A   of the shape of the continent.
    B   it is surrounded by a frozen sea.
    C   it is an extremely dry continent.

26 Dr Merrywhether thinks Antarctica was part of another continent because

    A   he has done his own research in the area.
    B   there is geological evidence of this.
    C   it is very close to South America.

Questions 27 and 28

Complete the table below.

*Write **ONE WORD AND/OR TWO NUMBERS** for each answer.*

ANTARCTIC TREATY

Date	Event
1870	*Polar Research meeting*
27 .... to	*1st International Polar Year*
1957	*Antarctic Treaty was proposed*
1959	*Antarctic Treaty was **28** ....*

Questions 29 and 30

*Choose **TWO** letters, A–E.*

*Which **TWO** achievements of the Antarctic Treaty are mentioned by the speakers?*

    A   no military use
    B   animals protected
    C   historic sites preserved
    D   no nuclear testing
    E   fishing rights protected

SECTION 4   *Questions 31–40*

Questions 31–35

*Choose the correct letter, **A**, **B** or **C**.*

Left and Right Handedness in Sport

31   Anita first felt the Matthews article was of value when she realised

    A   how it would help her difficulties with left-handedness.
    B   the relevance of connections he made with music.
    C   the impressive size of his research project.

32   Anita feels that the findings on handedness will be of value in

    A   helping sportspeople identify their weaknesses.
    B   aiding sportspeople as they plan tactics for each game.
    C   developing suitable training programmes for sportspeople.

33   Anita feels that most sports coaches

    A   know nothing about the influence of handedness.
    B   focus on the wrong aspects of performance.
    C   underestimate what science has to offer sport.

34   A German study showed there was greater 'mixed handedness' in musicians who

    A   started playing instruments in early youth.
    B   play a string instrument such as the violin.
    C   practise a great deal on their instrument.

35   Studies on ape behaviour show that

    A   apes which always use the same hand to get food are most successful.
    B   apes have the same proportion of left- and right-handers as humans.
    C   more apes are left-handed than right-handed.

Questions 36–40

Complete the table below.

Write ONE WORD AND/OR A NUMBER for each answer.

Sport	Best laterality	Comments
Hockey	mixed laterality	• hockey stick has to be used in **36** .... • mixed-handed players found to be much more **37** .... than others
Tennis	single laterality	• gives a larger relevant field of **38** .... • cross-lateral players make **39** .... too late
Gymnastics	cross laterality	• gymnasts' **40** .... is important for performances

READING

READING PASSAGE 1

*You should spend about 20 minutes on **Questions 1–13**, which are based on Reading Passage 1 below.*

Why pagodas don't fall down

In a land swept by typhoons and shaken by earthquakes, how have Japan's tallest and seemingly flimsiest old buildings – 500 or so wooden pagodas – remained standing for centuries? Records show that only two have collapsed during the past 1400 years. Those that have disappeared were destroyed by fire as a result of lightning or civil war. The disastrous Hanshin earthquake in 1995 killed 6,400 people, toppled elevated highways, flattened office blocks and devastated the port area of Kobe. Yet it left the magnificent five-storey pagoda at the Toji temple in nearby Kyoto unscathed, though it levelled a number of buildings in the neighbourhood.

Japanese scholars have been mystified for ages about why these tall, slender buildings are so stable. It was only thirty years ago that the building industry felt confident enough to erect office blocks of steel and reinforced concrete that had more than a dozen floors. With its special shock absorbers to dampen the effect of sudden sideways movements from an earthquake, the thirty-six-storey Kasumigaseki building in central Tokyo – Japan's first skyscraper – was considered a masterpiece of modern engineering when it was built in 1968.

Yet in 826, with only pegs and wedges to keep his wooden structure upright, the master builder Kobodaishi had no hesitation in sending his majestic Toji pagoda soaring fifty-five metres into the sky – nearly half as high as the Kasumigaseki skyscraper built some eleven centuries later. Clearly, Japanese carpenters of the day knew a few tricks about allowing a building to sway and settle itself rather than fight nature's forces. But what sort of tricks?

The multi-storey pagoda came to Japan from China in the sixth century. As in China, they were first introduced with Buddhism and were attached to important temples. The Chinese built their pagodas in brick or stone, with inner staircases, and used them in later centuries mainly as watchtowers. When the pagoda reached Japan, however, its architecture was freely adapted to local conditions – they were built less high, typically five rather than nine storeys, made mainly of wood and the staircase was dispensed with because the Japanese pagoda did not have any practical use but became more of an art object. Because of the typhoons that batter Japan in the summer, Japanese builders learned to extend the eaves of buildings further beyond the walls. This prevents rainwater gushing down the walls. Pagodas in China and Korea have nothing like the overhang that is found on pagodas in Japan.

The roof of a Japanese temple building can be made to overhang the sides of the structure by fifty per cent or more of the building's overall width. For the same reason, the builders of Japanese pagodas seem to have further increased their weight by choosing to cover these extended eaves not with the porcelain tiles of many Chinese pagodas but with much heavier earthenware tiles.

But this does not totally explain the great resilience of Japanese pagodas. Is the answer that, like a tall pine tree, the Japanese pagoda – with its massive trunk-like central pillar known as *shinbashira* – simply flexes and sways during a typhoon or earthquake? For centuries, many thought so. But the answer is not so simple because the startling thing is that the *shinbashira* actually carries no load at all. In fact, in some pagoda designs, it does not even rest on the ground, but is suspended from the top of the pagoda – hanging loosely down through the middle of the building. The weight of the building is supported entirely by twelve outer and four inner columns.

And what is the role of the *shinbashira*, the central pillar? The best way to understand the *shinbashira's* role is to watch a video made by Shuzo Ishida, a structural engineer at Kyoto Institute of Technology. Mr Ishida, known to his students as 'Professor Pagoda' because of his passion to understand the pagoda, has built a series of models and tested them on a 'shake-table' in his laboratory. In short, the *shinbashira* was acting like an enormous stationary pendulum. The ancient craftsmen, apparently without the assistance of very advanced mathematics, seemed to grasp the principles that were, more than a thousand years later, applied in the construction of Japan's first skyscraper. What those early craftsmen had found by trial and error was that under pressure a pagoda's loose stack of floors could be made to slither to and fro independent of one another. Viewed from the side, the pagoda seemed to be doing a snake dance – with each consecutive floor moving in the opposite direction to its neighbours above and below. The *shinbashira*, running up through a hole in the centre of the building, constrained individual storeys from moving too far because, after moving a certain distance, they banged into it, transmitting energy away along the column.

Another strange feature of the Japanese pagoda is that, because the building tapers, with each successive floor plan being smaller than the one below, none of the vertical pillars that carry the weight of the building is connected to its corresponding pillar above. In other words, a five-storey pagoda contains not even one pillar that travels right up through the building to carry the structural loads from the top to the bottom. More surprising is the fact that the individual storeys of a Japanese pagoda, unlike their counterparts elsewhere, are not actually connected to each other. They are simply stacked one on top of another like a pile of hats. Interestingly, such a design would not be permitted under current Japanese building regulations.

And the extra-wide eaves? Think of them as a tightrope walker's balancing pole. The bigger the mass at each end of the pole, the easier it is for the tightrope walker to maintain his or her balance. The same holds true for a pagoda. 'With the eaves extending out on all sides like balancing poles,' says Mr Ishida, 'the building responds to even the most powerful jolt of an earthquake with a graceful swaying, never an abrupt shaking.' Here again, Japanese master builders of a thousand years ago anticipated concepts of modern structural engineering.

Questions 1–4

Do the following statements agree with the claims of the writer in Reading Passage 1?

In boxes 1–4 on your answer sheet, write

> **YES**   *if the statement agrees with the claims of the writer*
> **NO**   *if the statement contradicts the claims of the writer*
> **NOT GIVEN** *if it is impossible to say what the writer thinks about this*

1   Only two Japanese pagodas have collapsed in 1400 years.

2   The Hanshin earthquake of 1995 destroyed the pagoda at the Toji temple.

3   The other buildings near the Toji pagoda had been built in the last 30 years.

4   The builders of pagodas knew how to absorb some of the power produced by severe weather conditions.

Questions 5–10

Classify the following as typical of

> **A**   both Chinese and Japanese pagodas
> **B**   only Chinese pagodas
> **C**   only Japanese pagodas

*Write the correct letter, **A**, **B** or **C**, in boxes 5–10 on your answer sheet.*

5   easy interior access to top

6   tiles on eaves

7   use as observation post

8   size of eaves up to half the width of the building

9   original religious purpose

10 floors fitting loosely over each other

Questions 11–13

*Choose the correct letter, **A**, **B**, **C** or **D**.*

Write the correct letter in boxes 11–13 on your answer sheet.

11   In a Japanese pagoda, the *shinbashira*

    A   bears the full weight of the building.
    B   bends under pressure like a tree.
    C   connects the floors with the foundations.
    D   stops the floors moving too far.

12   Shuzo Ishida performs experiments in order to

    A   improve skyscraper design.
    B   be able to build new pagodas.
    C   learn about the dynamics of pagodas.
    D   understand ancient mathematics.

13   The storeys of a Japanese pagoda are

    A   linked only by wood.
    B   fastened only to the central pillar.
    C   fitted loosely on top of each other.
    D   joined by special weights.

READING PASSAGE 2

*You should spend about 20 minutes on **Questions 14–26**, which are based on Reading Passage 2 below.*

The True Cost of Food

A For more than forty years the cost of food has been rising. It has now reached a point where a growing number of people believe that it is far too high, and that bringing it down will be one of the great challenges of the twenty first century. That cost, however, is not in immediate cash. In the West at least, most food is now far cheaper to buy in relative terms than it was in 1960. The cost is in the collateral damage of the very methods of food production that have made the food cheaper: in the pollution of water, the enervation of soil, the destruction of wildlife, the harm to animal welfare and the threat to human health caused by modern industrial agriculture.

B First mechanisation, then mass use of chemical fertilisers and pesticides, then monocultures, then battery rearing of livestock, and now genetic engineering – the onward march of intensive farming has seemed unstoppable in the last half-century, as the yields of produce have soared. But the damage it has caused has been colossal. In Britain, for example, many of our best-loved farmland birds, such as the skylark, the grey partridge, the lapwing and the corn bunting, have vanished from huge stretches of countryside, as have even more wild flowers and insects. This is a direct result of the way we have produced our food in the last four decades. Thousands of miles of hedgerows, thousands of ponds, have disappeared from the landscape. The faecal filth of salmon farming has driven wild salmon from many of the sea lochs and rivers of Scotland. Natural soil fertility is dropping in many areas because of continuous industrial fertiliser and pesticide use, while the growth of algae is increasing in lakes because of the fertiliser run-off.

C Put it all together and it looks like a battlefield, but consumers rarely make the connection at the dinner table. That is mainly because the costs of all this damage are what economists refer to as externalities: they are outside the main transaction, which is for example producing and selling a field of wheat, and are borne directly by neither producers nor consumers. To many, the costs may not even appear to be financial at all, but merely aesthetic – a terrible shame, but nothing to do with money. And anyway they, as consumers of food, certainly aren't paying for it, are they?

D But the costs to society can actually be quantified and, when added up, can amount to staggering sums. A remarkable exercise in doing this has been carried out by one of the world's leading thinkers on the future of agriculture, Professor Jules Pretty, Director of the Centre for Environment and Society at the University of Essex. Professor Pretty and his colleagues calculated the externalities of British agriculture for one particular year. They added up the costs of repairing the damage it caused, and came up with a total figure of £2,343m. This is equivalent to £208 for every hectare of arable land and permanent pasture, almost as much again as the total government and EU spend on British farming in that year. And according to Professor Pretty, it was a conservative estimate.

E The costs included: £120m for removal of pesticides; £16m for removal of nitrates; £55m for removal of phosphates and soil; £23m for the removal of the bug cryptosporidium from drinking water by water companies; £125m for damage to wildlife habitats, hedgerows and dry stone walls; £1,113m from emissions of gases likely to contribute to climate change; £106m from soil erosion and organic carbon losses; £169m from food poisoning; and £607m from cattle disease. Professor Pretty draws a simple but memorable conclusion from all this: our food bills are actually threefold. We are paying for our supposedly cheaper food in three separate ways: once over the counter, secondly through our taxes, which provide the enormous subsidies propping up modern intensive farming, and thirdly to clean up the mess that modern farming leaves behind.

F So can the true cost of food be brought down? Breaking away from industrial agriculture as the solution to hunger may be very hard for some countries, but in Britain, where the immediate need to supply food is less urgent, and the costs and the damage of intensive farming have been clearly seen, it may be more feasible. The government needs to create sustainable, competitive and diverse farming and food sectors, which will contribute to a thriving and sustainable rural economy, and advance environmental, economic, health, and animal welfare goals.

G But if industrial agriculture is to be replaced, what is a viable alternative? Professor Pretty feels that organic farming would be too big a jump in thinking and in practices for many farmers. Furthermore, the price premium would put the produce out of reach of many poorer consumers. He is recommending the immediate introduction of a 'Greener Food Standard', which would push the market towards more sustainable environmental practices than the current norm, while not requiring the full commitment to organic production. Such a standard would comprise agreed practices for different kinds of farming, covering agrochemical use, soil health, land management, water and energy use, food safety and animal health. It could go a long way, he says, to shifting consumers as well as farmers towards a more sustainable system of agriculture.

Questions 14–17

Reading Passage 2 has seven paragraphs, **A–G**.

Which paragraph contains the following information?

*Write the correct letter, **A–G**, in boxes 14–17 on your answer sheet.*

NB   *You may use any letter more than once.*

14   a cost involved in purifying domestic water

15   the stages in the development of the farming industry

16   the term used to describe hidden costs

17   one effect of chemicals on water sources

Questions 18–21

Do the following statements agree with the claims of the writer in Reading Passage 2?

In boxes 18–21 on your answer sheet, write

> **YES**   *if the statement agrees with the claims of the writer*
> **NO**   *if the statement contradicts the claims of the writer*
> **NOT GIVEN**   *if it is impossible to say what the writer thinks about this*

18   Several species of wildlife in the British countryside are declining.

19   The taste of food has deteriorated in recent years.

20   The financial costs of environmental damage are widely recognised.

21   One of the costs calculated by Professor Pretty was illness caused by food.

Questions 22–26

Complete the summary below.

*Choose **NO MORE THAN THREE WORDS** from the passage for each answer.*

Write your answers in boxes 22–26 on your answer sheet.

Professor Pretty concludes that our **22** .... are higher than most people realise, because we make three different types of payment. He feels it is realistic to suggest that Britain should reduce its reliance on **23** .... Although most farmers would be unable to adapt to **24** ...., Professor Pretty wants the government to initiate change by establishing what he refers to as a **25** .... He feels this would help to change the attitudes of both **26** ....and ....

READING PASSAGE 3

*You should spend about 20 minutes on **Questions 27–40**, which are based on Reading Passage 3 on the following pages.*

Questions 27–30

Reading Passage 3 has six sections, **A–F**.

*Choose the correct heading for sections **B**, **C**, **E** and **F** from the list of headings below.*

*Write the correct number, **i–xi**, in boxes **27–30** on your answer sheet.*

List of Headings
i MIRTP as a future model
ii Identifying the main transport problems
iii Preference for motorised vehicles
iv Government authorities' instructions
v Initial improvements in mobility and transport modes
vi Request for improved transport in Makete
vii Transport improvements in the northern part of the district
viii Improvements in the rail network
ix Effects of initial MIRTP measures
x Co-operation of district officials
xi Role of wheelbarrows and donkeys

Example	*Answer*
Section **A**	**vi**

27   Section **B**

28   Section **C**

Example	*Answer*
Section **D**	**ix**

29   Section **E**

30   Section **F**

Makete Integrated Rural Transport Project

Section A

The disappointing results of many conventional road transport projects in Africa led some experts to rethink the strategy by which rural transport problems were to be tackled at the beginning of the 1980s. A request for help in improving the availability of transport within the remote Makete District of south-western Tanzania presented the opportunity to try a new approach.

The concept of 'integrated rural transport' was adopted in the task of examining the transport needs of the rural households in the district. The objective was to reduce the time and effort needed to obtain access to essential goods and services through an improved rural transport system. The underlying assumption was that the time saved would be used instead for activities that would improve the social and economic development of the communities. The Makete Integrated Rural Transport Project (MIRTP) started in 1985 with financial support from the Swiss Development Corporation and was co-ordinated with the help of the Tanzanian government.

Section B

When the project began, Makete District was virtually totally isolated during the rainy season. The regional road was in such bad shape that access to the main towns was impossible for about three months of the year. Road traffic was extremely rare within the district, and alternative means of transport were restricted to donkeys in the north of the district. People relied primarily on the paths, which were slippery and dangerous during the rains.

Before solutions could be proposed, the problems had to be understood. Little was known about the transport demands of the rural households, so Phase I, between December 1985 and December 1987, focused on research. The socio-economic survey of more than 400 households in the district indicated that a household in Makete spent, on average, seven hours a day on transporting themselves and their goods, a figure which seemed extreme but which has also been obtained in surveys in other rural areas in Africa. Interesting facts regarding transport were found: 95% was on foot; 80% was within the locality; and 70% was related to the collection of water and firewood and travelling to grinding mills.

Section C

Having determined the main transport needs, possible solutions were identified which might reduce the time and burden. During Phase II, from January to February 1991, a number of approaches were implemented in an effort to improve mobility and access to transport.

An improvement of the road network was considered necessary to ensure the import and export of goods to the district. These improvements were carried out using methods that were heavily dependent on labour. In addition to the improvement of roads, these methods provided training in the operation of a mechanical workshop and bus and truck services. However, the difference from the conventional approach was that this time consideration was given to local transport needs outside the road network.

Most goods were transported along the paths that provide short-cuts up and down the hillsides, but the paths were a real safety risk and made the journey on foot even more arduous. It made sense to improve the paths by building steps, handrails and footbridges.

It was uncommon to find means of transport that were more efficient than walking but less technologically advanced than motor vehicles. The use of bicycles was constrained by their high cost and the lack of available spare parts. Oxen were not used at all but donkeys were used by a few households in the northern part of the district. MIRTP focused on what would be most appropriate for the inhabitants of Makete in terms of what was available, how much they could afford and what they were willing to accept.

After careful consideration, the project chose the promotion of donkeys – a donkey costs less than a bicycle – and the introduction of a locally manufacturable wheelbarrow.

Section D

At the end of Phase II, it was clear that the selected approaches to Makete's transport problems had had different degrees of success. Phase III, from March 1991 to March 1993, focused on the refinement and institutionalisation of these activities.

The road improvements and accompanying maintenance system had helped make the district centre accessible throughout the year. Essential goods from outside the district had become more readily available at the market, and prices did not fluctuate as much as they had done before.

Paths and secondary roads were improved only at the request of communities who were willing to participate in construction and maintenance. However, the improved paths impressed the inhabitants, and requests for assistance greatly increased soon after only a few improvements had been completed.

The efforts to improve the efficiency of the existing transport services were not very successful because most of the motorised vehicles in the district broke down and there were no resources to repair them. Even the introduction of low-cost means of transport was difficult because of the general poverty of the district. The locally manufactured wheelbarrows were still too expensive for all but a few of the households. Modifications to the original design by local carpenters cut production time and costs. Other local carpenters have been trained in the new design so that they can respond to requests. Nevertheless, a locally produced wooden wheelbarrow which costs around 5000 Tanzanian shillings (less than US$20) in Makete, and is about one quarter the cost of a metal wheelbarrow, is still too expensive for most people.

Donkeys, which were imported to the district, have become more common and contribute, in particular, to the transportation of crops and goods to market. Those who have bought donkeys are mainly from richer households but, with an increased supply through local breeding, donkeys should become more affordable. Meanwhile, local initiatives are promoting the renting out of the existing donkeys.

It should be noted, however, that a donkey, which at 20,000 Tanzanian shillings costs less than a bicycle, is still an investment equal to an average household's income over half a year. This clearly illustrates the need for supplementary measures if one wants to assist the rural poor.

Section E

It would have been easy to criticise the MIRTP for using in the early phases a 'top-down' approach, in which decisions were made by experts and officials before being handed down to communities, but it was necessary to start the process from the level of the governmental authorities of the district. It would have been difficult to respond to the requests of villagers and other rural inhabitants without the support and understanding of district authorities.

Section F

Today, nobody in the district argues about the importance of improved paths and inexpensive means of transport. But this is the result of dedicated work over a long period, particularly from the officers in charge of community development. They played an essential role in raising awareness and interest among the rural communities.

The concept of integrated rural transport is now well established in Tanzania, where a major program of rural transport is just about to start. The experiences from Makete will help in this initiative, and Makete District will act as a reference for future work.

Questions 31–35

Do the following statements agree with the claims of the writer in Reading Passage 3?

In boxes 31–35 on your answer sheet, write

YES	*if the statement agrees with the claims of the writer*
NO	*if the statement contradicts the claims of the writer*
NOT GIVEN	*if it is impossible to say what the writer thinks about this*

31   MIRTP was divided into five phases.

32   Prior to the start of MIRTP the Makete district was almost inaccessible during the rainy season.

33   Phase I of MIRTP consisted of a survey of household expenditure on transport.

34   The survey concluded that one-fifth or 20% of the household transport requirement as outside the local area.

35   MIRTP hoped to improve the movement of goods from Makete district to the country's capital.

Questions 36–39

*Complete each sentence with the correct ending, **A–J**, below.*

*Write the correct letter, **A–J**, in boxes 36–39 on your answer sheet.*

36 Construction of footbridges, steps and handrails

37 Frequent breakdown of buses and trucks in Makete

38 The improvement of secondary roads and paths

39 The isolation of Makete for part of the year

A	provided the people of Makete with experience in running bus and truck services.
B	was especially successful in the northern part of the district.
C	differed from earlier phases in that the community became less actively involved.
D	improved paths used for transport up and down hillsides.
E	was no longer a problem once the roads had been improved.
F	cost less than locally made wheelbarrows.
G	was done only at the request of local people who were willing to lend a hand.
H	was at first considered by MIRTP to be affordable for the people of the district.
I	hindered attempts to make the existing transport services more efficient.
J	was thought to be the most important objective of Phase III.

Question 40

*Choose the correct letter, **A**, **B**, **C** or **D**.*

Write the correct letter in box 40 on your answer sheet.

Which of the following phrases best describes the main aim of Reading Passage 3?

    A to suggest that projects such as MIRTP are needed in other countries

    B to describe how MIRTP was implemented and how successful it was

    C to examine how MIRTP promoted the use of donkeys

    D to warn that projects such as MIRTP are likely to have serious problems

WRITING

WRITING TASK 1

You should spend about 20 minutes on this task.

> *The graph below shows the consumption of fish and some different kinds of meat in a European country between 1979 and 2004.*
>
> *Summarise the information by selecting and reporting the main features, and make comparisons where relevant.*

Write at least 150 words.

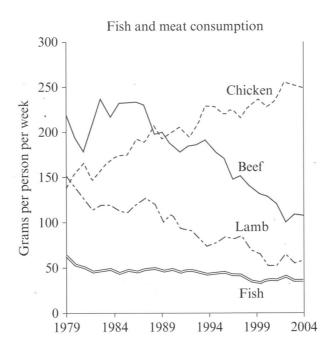

WRITING TASK 2

You should spend about 40 minutes on this task.

Write about the following topic:

Some people believe that there should be fixed punishments for each type of crime. Others, however, argue that the circumstances of an individual crime, and the motivation for committing it, should always be taken into account when deciding on the punishment.

Discuss both these views and give your own opinion.

Give reasons for your answer and include any relevant examples from your own knowledge or experience.

Write at least 250 words.

SPEAKING

PART 1

The examiner asks the candidate about him/herself, his/her home, work or studies and other familiar topics.

EXAMPLE

Laughing

- What kinds of thing make you laugh?
- Do you like making other people laugh? [Why/Why not?]
- Do you think it's important for people to laugh? [Why/Why not?]
- Is laughing the same as feeling happy, do you think? [Why/Why not?]

PART 2

> **Describe an idea you had for improving something at work or college.**
>
> **You should say:**
>   **when and where you had your idea**
>   **what your idea was**
>   **who you told about your idea**
> **and explain why you thought your idea would make an improvement.**

You will have to talk about the topic for one to two minutes.
You have one minute to think about what you are going to say.
You can make some notes to help you if you wish.

PART 3

Discussion topics:

Ideas and education

Example questions:
Some people think that education should be about memorising the important ideas of the past. Do you agree or disagree? Why?
Should education encourage students to have their own new ideas? Why?
How do you think teachers could help students to develop and share their own ideas?

Ideas in the workplace

Example questions:
Should employers encourage their workers to have new ideas about improving the company? Why?
Do you think people sometimes dislike ideas just because they are new? Why?
What is more difficult: having new ideas or putting them into practice? Which is more important for a successful company?

Test 3

SECTION 1   *Questions 1–10*

Questions 1 and 2

Complete the notes below.

*Write **NO MORE THAN THREE WORDS AND/OR A NUMBER** for each answer.*

Example	Answer
Type of job required:	Part-time

Student is studying **1** ....

Student is in the **2** .... year of the course.

Questions 3–5

Complete the table below.

*Write **NO MORE THAN TWO WORDS** for each answer.*

Position Available	Where	Problem
Receptionist	in the **3**	evening lectures
4	in the Child Care Centre	too early
Clerical Assistant	in the **5**	evening lectures

Questions 6–10

Complete the form below.

Write **NO MORE THAN THREE WORDS AND/OR A NUMBER** *for each answer.*

STUDENT DETAILS	
Name:	Anita Newman
Address:	6 .... Room No. 7 ....
Other skills:	Speaks some Japanese
Position available:	8 .... at the English Language Centre
Duties:	Respond to enquiries and 9 ....
Time of interview:	Friday at 10 .... a.m.

SECTION 2   *Questions 11–20*

Questions 11–16

*Choose the correct letter, **A**, **B** or **C**.*

SPONSORED WALKING HOLIDAY

11   On the holiday, you will be walking for

    A   6 days.
    B   8 days.
    C   10 days.

12   What proportion of the sponsorship money goes to charity?

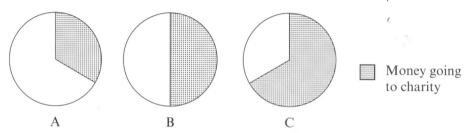

    A   B   C

Money going to charity

13   Each walker's sponsorship money goes to one

    A   student.
    B   teacher.
    C   school.

14   When you start the trek you must be

    A   interested in getting fit.
    B   already quite fit.
    C   already very fit.

15   As you walk you will carry

    A   all of your belongings.
    B   some of your belongings.
    C   none of your belongings.

16   The Semira Region has a long tradition of

    A   making carpets.
    B   weaving blankets.
    C   carving wood.

Questions 17–20

Complete the form below.

Write ONE WORD ONLY for each answer.

ITINERARY	
Day 1	arrive in Kishba
Day 2	rest day
Day 3	spend all day in a **17** ....
Day 4	visit a school
Day 5	rest day
Day 6	see a **18** ....with old carvings
Day 7	rest day
Day 8	swim in a **19** ....
Day 9	visit a **20** ....
Day 10	depart from Kishba

SECTION 3   *Questions 21–30*

Questions 21 and 22

Complete the notes below.

*Write **ONE WORD AND/OR A NUMBER** for each answer.*

OCEAN RESEARCH

The Robotic Float Project

- Float is shaped like a **21** ....
- Scientists from **22** .... have worked on the project so far

Questions 23–25

Complete the diagram below.

*Write **ONE WORD AND/OR A NUMBER** for each answer.*

THE OPERATIONAL CYCLE

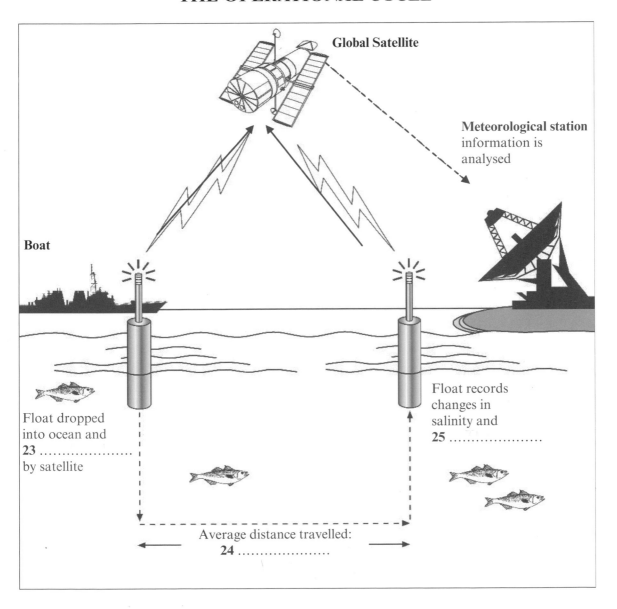

Global Satellite

Meteorological station
information is
analysed

Boat

Float records
changes in
salinity and
25 ....

Float dropped
into ocean and
23 ....
by satellite

Average distance travelled:
24 ....

Questions 26–30

In what time period can data from the float projects help with the following things?

*Write the correct letter, **A**, **B** or **C**, next to questions 26–30.*

A At present
B In the near future
C In the long-term future

26	understanding of El Niño	....
27	understanding of climate change	....
28	naval rescues	....
29	sustainable fishing practices	....
30	crop selection	....

SECTION 4   *Questions 31–40*

Questions 31–34

*Choose the correct letter, **A**, **B** or **C**.*

Hotels and the tourist industry

31   According to the speaker, how might a guest feel when staying in a luxury hotel?

    A   impressed with the facilities
    B   depressed by the experience
    C   concerned at the high costs

32   According to recent research, luxury hotels overlook the need to

    A   provide for the demands of important guests.
    B   create a comfortable environment.
    C   offer an individual and personal welcome.

33   The company focused their research on

    A   a wide variety of hotels.
    B   large, luxury hotel chains.
    C   exotic holiday hotels.

34   What is the impact of the outside environment on a hotel guest?

    A   It has a considerable effect.
    B   It has a very limited effect.
    C   It has no effect whatsoever.

Questions 35–40

Complete the notes below.

Write **ONE WORD ONLY** *for each answer.*

A company providing luxury serviced apartments aims to:

- cater specifically for **35** .... travellers

- provide a stylish **36** .... for guests to use

- set a trend throughout the **37** .... which becomes permanent

Traditional holiday hotels attract people by:

- offering the chance to **38** .... their ordinary routine life

- making sure that they are cared for in all respects – like a **39** ....

- leaving small treats in their rooms – e.g. cosmetics or **40** ....

READING

READING PASSAGE 1

*You should spend about 20 minutes on **Questions 1–13**, which are based on Reading Passage 1 below.*

Ant Intelligence

When we think of intelligent members of the animal kingdom, the creatures that spring immediately to mind are apes and monkeys. But in fact the social lives of some members of the insect kingdom are sufficiently complex to suggest more than a hint of intelligence.

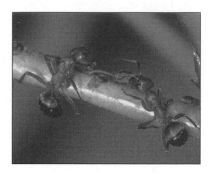

Among these, the world of the ant has come in for considerable scrutiny lately, and the idea that ants demonstrate sparks of cognition has certainly not been rejected by those involved in these investigations.

Ants store food, repel attackers and use chemical signals to contact one another in case of attack. Such chemical communication can be compared to the human use of visual and auditory channels (as in religious chants, advertising images and jingles, political slogans and martial music) to arouse and propagate moods and attitudes. The biologist Lewis Thomas wrote, 'Ants are so much like human beings as to be an embarrassment. They farm fungi, raise aphids* as livestock, launch armies to war, use chemical sprays to alarm and confuse enemies, capture slaves, engage in child labour, exchange information ceaselessly. They do everything but watch television.'

However, in ants there is no cultural transmission – everything must be encoded in the genes – whereas in humans the opposite is true. Only basic instincts are carried in the genes of a newborn baby, other skills being learned from others in the community as the child grows up. It may seem that this cultural continuity gives us a huge advantage over ants. They have never mastered fire nor progressed. Their fungus farming and aphid herding crafts are sophisticated when compared to the agricultural skills of humans five thousand years ago but have been totally overtaken by modern human agribusiness.

Or have they? The farming methods of ants are at least sustainable. They do not ruin environments or use enormous amounts of energy. Moreover, recent evidence suggests that the crop farming of ants may be more sophisticated and adaptable than was thought.

Ants were farmers fifty million years before humans were. Ants can't digest the cellulose in leaves – but some fungi can. The ants therefore cultivate these fungi in their nests, bringing them leaves to feed on, and then

---

* aphids: small insects of a different species from ants

use them as a source of food. Farmer ants secrete antibiotics to control other fungi that might act as 'weeds', and spread waste to fertilise the crop.

It was once thought that the fungus that ants cultivate was a single type that they had propagated, essentially unchanged from the distant past. Not so. Ulrich Mueller of Maryland and his colleagues genetically screened 862 different types of fungi taken from ants' nests. These turned out to be highly diverse: it seems that ants are continually domesticating new species. Even more impressively, DNA analysis of the fungi suggests that the ants improve or modify the fungi by regularly swapping and sharing strains with neighbouring ant colonies.

Whereas prehistoric man had no exposure to urban lifestyles – the forcing house of intelligence – the evidence suggests that ants have lived in urban settings for close on a hundred million years, developing and maintaining underground cities of specialised chambers and tunnels.

When we survey Mexico City, Tokyo, Los Angeles, we are amazed at what has been accomplished by humans. Yet Hoelldobler and Wilson's magnificent work for ant lovers, *The Ants*, describes a supercolony of the ant *Formica yessensis* on the Ishikari Coast of Hokkaido. This 'megalopolis' was reported to be composed of 360 million workers and a million queens living in 4,500 interconnected nests across a territory of 2.7 square kilometres.

Such enduring and intricately meshed levels of technical achievement outstrip by far anything achieved by our distant ancestors. We hail as masterpieces the cave paintings in southern France and elsewhere, dating back some 20,000 years. Ant societies existed in something like their present form more than seventy million years ago. Beside this, prehistoric man looks technologically primitive. Is this then some kind of intelligence, albeit of a different kind?

Research conducted at Oxford, Sussex and Zürich Universities has shown that when desert ants return from a foraging trip, they navigate by integrating bearings and distances, which they continuously update in their heads. They combine the evidence of visual landmarks with a mental library of local directions, all within a framework which is consulted and updated. So ants can learn too.

And in a twelve-year programme of work, Ryabko and Reznikova have found evidence that ants can transmit very complex messages. Scouts who had located food in a maze returned to mobilise their foraging teams. They engaged in contact sessions, at the end of which the scout was removed in order to observe what her team might do. Often the foragers proceeded to the exact spot in the maze where the food had been. Elaborate precautions were taken to prevent the foraging team using odour clues. Discussion now centres on whether the route through the maze is communicated as a 'left-right' sequence of turns or as a 'compass bearing and distance' message.

During the course of this exhaustive study, Reznikova has grown so attached to her laboratory ants that she feels she knows them as individuals – even without the paint spots used to mark them. It's no surprise that Edward Wilson, in his essay, 'In the company of ants', advises readers who ask what to do with the ants in their kitchen to: 'Watch where you step. Be careful of little lives.'

Questions 1–6

Do the following statements agree with the information given in Reading Passage 1?

In boxes 1–6 on your answer sheet, write

TRUE	*if the statement agrees with the information*
FALSE	*if the statement contradicts the information*
NOT GIVEN	*if there is no information on this*

1 Ants use the same channels of communication as humans do.

2 City life is one factor that encourages the development of intelligence.

3 Ants can build large cities more quickly than humans do.

4 Some ants can find their way by making calculations based on distance and position.

5 In one experiment, foraging teams were able to use their sense of smell to find food.

6 The essay, 'In the company of ants', explores ant communication.

Questions 7–13

*Complete the summary using the list of words, **A–O**, below.*

*Write the correct letter, **A–O**, in boxes 7–13 on your answer sheet.*

Ants as farmers

Ants have sophisticated methods of farming, including herding livestock and growing crops, which are in many ways similar to those used in human agriculture. The ants cultivate a large number of different species of edible fungi which convert **7** .... into a form which they can digest. They use their own natural **8** .... as weed-killers and also use unwanted materials as **9** .... Genetic analysis shows they constantly upgrade these fungi by developing new species and by **10** .... species with neighbouring ant colonies. In fact, the farming methods of ants could be said to be more advanced than human agribusiness, since they use **11** .... methods, they do not affect the **12** .... and do not waste **13** ....

A aphids	**B** agricultural	**C** cellulose	**D** exchanging
E energy	**F** fertilizers	**G** food	**H** fungi
I growing	**J** interbreeding	**K** natural	**L** other species
M secretions	**N** sustainable	**O** environment	

READING PASSAGE 2

*You should spend about 20 minutes on **Questions 14–26**, which are based on Reading Passage 2 on the following pages.*

Questions 14–19

Reading Passage 2 has seven sections, **A–G**.

*Choose the correct headings for sections **A–F** from the list of headings below.*

*Write the correct number, **i–x**, in boxes 14–19 on your answer sheet.*

List of Headings

i	The results of the research into blood-variants
ii	Dental evidence
iii	Greenberg's analysis of the dental and linguistic evidence
iv	Developments in the methods used to study early population movements
v	Indian migration from Canada to the U.S.A.
vi	Further genetic evidence relating to the three-wave theory
vii	Long-standing questions about prehistoric migration to America
viii	Conflicting views of the three-wave theory, based on non-genetic evidence
ix	Questions about the causes of prehistoric migration to America
x	How analysis of blood-variants measures the closeness of the relationship between different populations

---

14   Section **A**

15   Section **B**

16   Section **C**

17   Section **D**

18   Section **E**

19   Section **F**

Example	*Answer*
Section **G**	**viii**

Population movements and genetics

A Study of the origins and distribution of human populations used to be based on archaeological and fossil evidence. A number of techniques developed since the 1950s, however, have placed the study of these subjects on a sounder and more objective footing. The best information on early population movements is now being obtained from the 'archaeology of the living body', the clues to be found in genetic material.

B Recent work on the problem of when people first entered the Americas is an example of the value of these new techniques. North-east Asia and Siberia have long been accepted as the launching ground for the first human colonisers of the New World[1]. But was there one major wave of migration across the Bering Strait into the Americas, or several? And when did this event, or events, take place? In recent years, new clues have come from research into genetics, including the distribution of genetic markers in modern Native Americans[2].

C An important project, led by the biological anthropologist Robert Williams, focused on the variants (called Gm allotypes) of one particular protein – immunoglobin G – found in the fluid portion of human blood. All proteins 'drift', or produce variants, over the generations, and members of an interbreeding human population will share a set of such variants. Thus, by comparing the Gm allotypes of two different populations (e.g. two Indian tribes), one can establish their genetic 'distance', which itself can be calibrated to give an indication of the length of time since these populations last interbred.

D Williams and his colleagues sampled the blood of over 5,000 American Indians in western North America during a twenty-year period. They found that their Gm allotypes could be divided into two groups, one of which also corresponded to the genetic typing of Central and South American Indians. Other tests showed that the Inuit (or Eskimo) and Aleut[3] formed a third group. From this evidence it was deduced that there had been three major waves of migration across the Bering Strait. The first, Paleo-Indian, wave more than 15,000 years ago was ancestral to all Central and South American Indians. The second wave, about 14,000–12,000 years ago, brought Na-Dene hunters, ancestors of the Navajo and Apache (who only migrated south from Canada about 600 or 700 years ago). The third wave, perhaps 10,000 or 9,000 years ago, saw the migration from North-east Asia of groups ancestral to the modern Eskimo and Aleut.

E How far does other research support these conclusions? Geneticist Douglas Wallace has studied mitochondrial DNA[4] in blood samples from three widely separated Native American groups: Pima-Papago Indians in Arizona, Maya Indians on the Yucatán peninsula, Mexico, and

---

[1] New World: the American continent, as opposed to the so-called Old World of Europe, Asia and Africa
[2] modern Native American: an American descended from the groups that were native to America
[3] Inuit and Aleut: two of the ethnic groups native to the northern regions of North America (i.e. northern Canada and Greenland)
[4] DNA: the substance in which genetic information is stored

Ticuna Indians in the Upper Amazon region of Brazil. As would have been predicted by Robert Williams's work, all three groups appear to be descended from the same ancestral (Paleo-Indian) population.

F   There are two other kinds of research that have thrown some light on the origins of the Native American population; they involve the study of teeth and of languages. The biological anthropologist Christy Turner is an expert in the analysis of changing physical characteristics in human teeth. He argues that tooth crowns and roots[5] have a high genetic component, minimally affected by environmental and other factors. Studies carried out by Turner of many thousands of New and Old World specimens, both ancient and modern, suggest that the majority of prehistoric Americans are linked to Northern Asian populations by crown and root traits such as incisor[6] shoveling (a scooping out on one or both surfaces of the tooth), single-rooted upper first premolars[6] and triple-rooted lower first molars[6].

According to Turner, this ties in with the idea of a single Paleo-Indian migration out of North Asia, which he sets at before 14,000 years ago by calibrating rates of dental micro-evolution. Tooth analyses also suggest that there were two later migrations of Na-Denes and Eskimo-Aleut.

G   The linguist Joseph Greenberg has, since the 1950s, argued that all Native American languages belong to a single 'Amerind' family, except for Na-Dene and Eskimo-Aleut – a view that gives credence to the idea of three main migrations. Greenberg is in a minority among fellow linguists, most of whom favour the notion of a great many waves of migration to account for the more than 1,000 languages spoken at one time by American Indians. But there is no doubt that the new genetic and dental evidence provides strong backing for Greenberg's view. Dates given for the migrations should nevertheless be treated with caution, except where supported by hard archaeological evidence.

---

[5] crown/root: parts of the tooth
[6] incisor/premolar/molar: kinds of teeth

Questions 20 and 21

The discussion of Williams's research indicates the periods at which early people are thought to have migrated along certain routes. There are six routes, **A–F**, marked on the map below.

Complete the table below.

*Write the correct letter, **A–F**, in boxes 20 and 21 on your answer sheet.*

Route	Period (number of years ago)
20	15,000 or more
21	600 to 700

Early Population Movement to the Americas

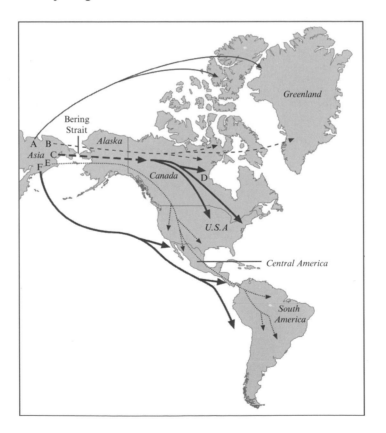

Questions 22–25

Reading Passage 2 refers to the three-wave theory of early migration to the Americas. It also suggests in which of these three waves the ancestors of various groups of modern native Americans first reached the continent.

Classify the groups named in the table below as originating from

    A   the first wave
    B   the second wave
    C   the third wave

*Write the correct letter, **A**, **B** or **C**, in boxes 22–25 on your answer sheet.*

Name of group	Wave number
Inuit	**22** ....
Apache	**23** ....
Pima-Papago	**24** ....
Ticuna	**25** ....

Question 26

*Choose the correct letter, **A**, **B**, **C** or **D**.*

Write the correct letter in box 26 on your answer sheet.

Christy Turner's research involved the examination of

    A   teeth from both prehistoric and modern Americans and Asians.
    B   thousands of people who live in either the New or the Old World.
    C   dental specimens from the majority of prehistoric Americans.
    D   the eating habits of American and Asian populations.

READING PASSAGE 3

*You should spend about 20 minutes on **Questions 27–40**, which are based on Reading Passage 3 below.*

Forests are one of the main elements of our natural heritage. The decline of Europe's forests over the last decade and a half has led to an increasing awareness and understanding of the serious imbalances which threaten them. European countries are becoming increasingly concerned by major threats to European forests, threats which know no frontiers other than those of geography or climate: air pollution, soil deterioration, the increasing number of forest fires and sometimes even the mismanagement of our woodland and forest heritage. There has been a growing awareness of the need for countries to get together to co-ordinate their policies. In December 1990, Strasbourg hosted the first Ministerial Conference on the protection of Europe's forests. The conference brought together 31 countries from both Western and Eastern Europe. The topics discussed included the co-ordinated study of the destruction of forests, as well as how to combat forest fires and the extension of European research programs on the forest ecosystem. The preparatory work for the conference had been undertaken at two meetings of experts. Their initial task was to decide which of the many forest problems of concern to Europe involved the largest number of countries and might be the subject of joint action. Those confined to particular geographical areas, such as countries bordering the Mediterranean or the Nordic countries therefore had to be discarded. However, this does not mean that in future they will be ignored.

As a whole, European countries see forests as performing a triple function: biological, economic and recreational. The first is to act as a 'green lung' for our planet; by means of photosynthesis, forests produce oxygen through the transformation of solar energy, thus fulfilling what for humans is the essential role of an immense, non-polluting power plant. At the same time, forests provide raw materials for human activities through their constantly renewed production of wood. Finally, they offer those condemned to spend five days a week in an urban environment an unrivalled area of freedom to unwind and take part in a range of leisure activities, such as hunting, riding and hiking. The economic importance of forests has been understood since the dawn of man – wood was the first fuel. The other aspects have been recognised only for a few centuries but they are becoming more and more important. Hence, there is a real concern throughout Europe about the damage to the forest environment which threatens these three basic roles.

The myth of the 'natural' forest has survived, yet there are effectively no remaining 'primary' forests in Europe. All European forests are artificial, having been adapted and exploited by man for thousands of years. This means that a forest policy is vital, that it must transcend national frontiers and generations of people, and that it must allow for the inevitable changes that take place in the forests, in needs, and hence in policy. The Strasbourg conference was one of the first events on such a scale to reach this conclusion. A general declaration was made that 'a central place in any ecologically coherent forest policy must be given to continuity over time and to the possible effects of unforeseen events, to ensure that the full potential of these forests is maintained'.

That general declaration was accompanied by six detailed resolutions to assist national policy-making. The first proposes the extension and systematisation of surveillance sites to monitor forest decline. Forest decline is still poorly understood but leads to the loss of a high proportion of a tree's needles or leaves. The entire continent and the majority of species are now affected: between 30% and 50% of the tree population. The condition appears to result from the cumulative effect of a number of factors, with atmospheric pollutants the principal culprits. Compounds of nitrogen and sulphur dioxide should be particularly closely watched. However, their effects are probably accentuated by climatic factors, such as drought and hard winters, or soil imbalances such as soil acidification, which damages the roots. The second resolution concentrates on the need to preserve the genetic diversity of European forests. The aim is to reverse the decline in the number of tree species or at least to preserve the 'genetic material' of all of them. Although forest fires do not affect all of Europe to the same extent, the amount of damage caused the experts to propose as the third resolution that the Strasbourg conference consider the establishment of a European databank on the subject. All information used in the development of national preventative policies would become generally available. The subject of the fourth resolution discussed by the ministers was mountain forests. In Europe, it is undoubtedly the mountain ecosystem which has changed most rapidly and is most at risk. A thinly scattered permanent population and development of leisure activities, particularly skiing, have resulted in significant long-term changes to the local ecosystems. Proposed developments include a preferential research program on mountain forests. The fifth resolution relaunched the European research network on the physiology of trees, called Eurosilva. Eurosilva should support joint European research on tree diseases and their physiological and biochemical aspects. Each country concerned could increase the number of scholarships and other financial support for doctoral theses and research projects in this area. Finally, the conference established the framework for a European research network on forest ecosystems. This would also involve harmonising activities in individual countries as well as identifying a number of priority research topics relating to the protection of forests. The Strasbourg conference's main concern was to provide for the future. This was the initial motivation, one now shared by all 31 participants representing 31 European countries. Their final text commits them to on-going discussion between government representatives with responsibility for forests.

Questions 27–33

Do the following statements agree with the information given in Reading Passage 3?

In boxes 27–33 on your answer sheet, write

>| **TRUE** | *if the statement agrees with the information* |
>| **FALSE** | *if the statement contradicts the information* |
>| **NOT GIVEN** | *if there is no information on this* |

27 Forest problems of Mediterranean countries are to be discussed at the next meeting of experts.

28 Problems in Nordic countries were excluded because they are outside the European Economic Community.

29 Forests are a renewable source of raw material.

30 The biological functions of forests were recognised only in the twentieth century.

31 Natural forests still exist in parts of Europe.

32 Forest policy should be limited by national boundaries.

33 The Strasbourg conference decided that a forest policy must allow for the possibility of change.

Questions 34–39

Look at the following statements issued by the conference.

*Which six of the following statements, **A–J**, refer to the resolutions that were issued?*

Match the statements with the appropriate resolutions (Questions 34–39).

*Write the correct letter, **A–J**, in boxes 34–39 on your answer sheet.*

A	All kinds of species of trees should be preserved.
B	Fragile mountain forests should be given priority in research programs.
C	The surviving natural forests of Europe do not need priority treatment.
D	Research is to be better co-ordinated throughout Europe.
E	Information on forest fires should be collected and shared.
F	Loss of leaves from trees should be more extensively and carefully monitored.
G	Resources should be allocated to research into tree diseases.
H	Skiing should be encouraged in thinly populated areas.
I	Soil imbalances such as acidification should be treated with compounds of nitrogen and sulphur.
J	Information is to be systematically gathered on any decline in the condition of forests.

34 Resolution 1

35 Resolution 2

36 Resolution 3

37 Resolution 4

38 Resolution 5

39 Resolution 6

Question 40

Choose the correct letter, **A**, **B**, **C** or **D**.

Write the correct letter in box 40 on your answer sheet.

40 What is the best title for Reading Passage 3?

    A The biological, economic and recreational role of forests

    B Plans to protect the forests of Europe

    C The priority of European research into ecosystems

    D Proposals for a world-wide policy on forest management

WRITING

WRITING TASK 1

You should spend about 20 minutes on this task.

The chart below shows information about changes in average house prices in five different cities between 1990 and 2002 compared with the average house prices in 1989.

Summarise the information by selecting and reporting the main features, and make comparisons where relevant.

Write at least 150 words.

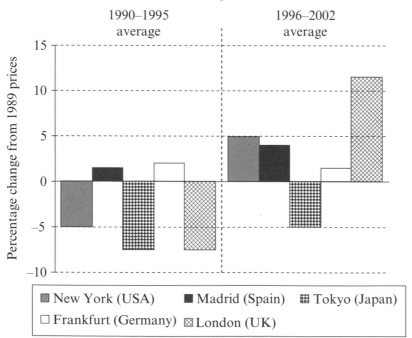

Percentage change in average house prices in five cities
1990–2002 compared with 1989

WRITING TASK 2

You should spend about 40 minutes on this task.

Write about the following topic:

> *As most people spend a major part of their adult life at work, job satisfaction is an important element of individual wellbeing.*
>
> *What factors contribute to job satisfaction?*
>
> *How realistic is the expectation of job satisfaction for all workers?*

Give reasons for your answer and include any relevant examples from your own knowledge or experience.

Write at least 250 words.

SPEAKING

PART 1

The examiner asks the candidate about him/herself, his/her home, work or studies and other familiar topics.

EXAMPLE

Cold weather

- Have you ever been in very cold weather? [When?]
- How often is the weather cold where you come from?
- Are some parts of your country colder than others? [Why?]
- Would you prefer to live in a hot place or a cold place? [Why?]

PART 2

> **Describe a competition (e.g. TV, college/work or sports competition) that you took part in.**
>
> **You should say:**
>   **what kind of competition it was and how you found out about it**
>   **what you had to do**
>   **what the prizes were**
> **and explain why you chose to take part in this competition.**

You will have to talk about the topic for one to two minutes.
You have one minute to think about what you are going to say.
You can make some notes to help you if you wish.

PART 3

Discussion topics:

Competitions in school

Example questions:
Why do you think some school teachers use competitions as class activities?
Do you think it is a good thing to give prizes to children who do well at school? Why?
Would you say that schools for young children have become more or less competitive since you were that age? Why?

Sporting competitions

Example questions:
What are the advantages and disadvantages of intensive training for young sportspeople?
Some people think that competition leads to a better performance from sports stars. Others think it just makes players feel insecure. What is your opinion?
Do you think that it is possible to become too competitive in sport? In what way?

Test 4

SECTION 1   *Questions 1–10*

Questions 1–6

Complete the form below.

Write **NO MORE THAN THREE WORDS AND/OR A NUMBER** *for each answer.*

HOMESTAY APPLICATION		
Example **Surname:**	*Answer* ....Yuichini.......	
First name:	1	
Sex:	female	**Nationality:** Japanese
Passport number:	2	**Age:** 28 years
Present address:	Room 21C, Willow College	
Length of homestay:	approx 3	
Course enrolled in:	4	
Family preferences:	no 5	
	no objection to 6	

Questions 7–10

Answer the questions below.

*Write **NO MORE THAN TWO WORDS** for each answer.*

7   What does the student particularly like to eat?   ....

8   What sport does the student play?   ....

9   What mode of transport does the student prefer?   ....

10 When will the student find out her homestay address?   ....

SECTION 2   *Questions 11–20*

Questions 11–14

Choose the correct letter, A, B or C.

11 What kind of tour is Sally leading?

    A   a bus tour
    B   a train tour
    C   a walking tour

12 The original buildings on the site were

    A   houses.
    B   industrial buildings.
    C   shops.

13 The local residents wanted to use the site for

    A   leisure.
    B   apartment blocks.
    C   a sports centre.

14 The Tower is at the centre of the

    A   nature reserve.
    B   formal gardens.
    C   Bicentennial Park.

Questions 15–17

Label the plan below.

Write NO MORE THAN TWO WORDS for each answer.

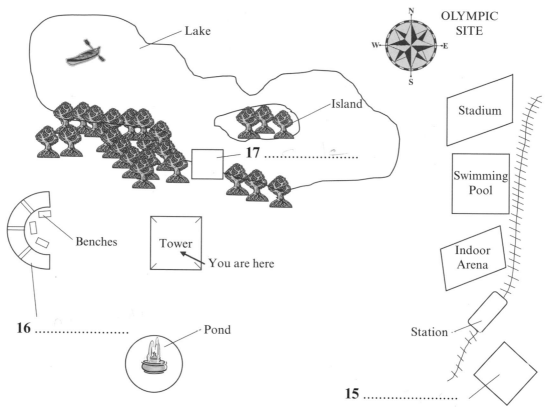

Questions 18–20

Complete the table below.

Write NO MORE THAN TWO WORDS for each answer.

Nature Reserve

Area	Facility	Activity
The Mangroves	boardwalk	**18** ....
Frog Pond	outdoor classroom	**19** ....
The Waterbird Refuge	**20**	bird watching

SECTION 3   *Questions 21–30*

Questions 21 and 22

Complete the sentences below.

*Write **NO MORE THAN ONE WORD AND/OR A NUMBER** for each answer.*

The presentation will last 15 minutes.

There will be **21** .... minutes for questions.

The presentation will not be **22** ....

Questions 23–26

What do the students decide about each topic for the geography presentation?

    A   They will definitely include this topic.
    B   They might include this topic.
    C   They will not include this topic.

*Write the correct letter, **A**, **B** or **C**, next to questions 23–26.*

23	Geographical Location	....
24	Economy	....
25	Overview of Education System	....
26	Role of English Language	....

Questions 27–30

Complete the table below.

Write **NO MORE THAN TWO WORDS** *for each answer.*

Information/visual aid	Where from?
Overhead projector	the **27** ....
Map of West Africa	the **28** ....
Map of the islands	a tourist brochure
Literacy figures	the **29** ....
30 .... on school places	as above

SECTION 4   *Questions 31–40*

Questions 31–33

Choose the correct letter, A, B or C.

Monosodium Glutamate (MSG)

31 The speaker says the main topic of the lecture is

  A   the history of monosodium glutamate.
  B   the way monosodium glutamate works.
  C   where monosodium glutamate is used.

32 In 1908, scientists in Japan

  A   made monosodium glutamate.
  B   began using kombu.
  C   identified glutamate.

33 What change occurred in the manufacture of glutamate in 1956?

  A   It began to be manufactured on a large scale.
  B   The Japanese began extracting it from natural sources.
  C   It became much more expensive to produce.

Questions 34–40

Complete the notes below.

*Write **NO MORE THAN TWO WORDS** for each answer.*

Monosodium Glutamate (MSG)

- MSG contains

    – glutamate (78.2%)

    – sodium (12.2%)

    – **34** .... (9.6%)

- Glutamate is found in foods that contain protein such as **35** .... and

    36 ....

- MSG is used in foods in many different parts of the world.

- In 1908 Kikunae Ikeda discovered a **37** ....

- Our ability to detect glutamate makes sense because it is so **38** ....

    naturally.

- John Prescott suggests that:

    – sweetness tells us that a food contains carbohydrates.

    – **39** .... tells us that a food contains toxins.

    – sourness tells us that a food is spoiled.

    – saltiness tells us that a food contains **40** ....

READING PASSAGE 1

*You should spend about 20 minutes on **Questions 1–13,** which are based on Reading Passage 1 below.*

Pulling strings to build pyramids

No one knows exactly how the pyramids were built. Marcus Chown reckons the answer could be 'hanging in the air'.

The pyramids of Egypt were built more than three thousand years ago, and no one knows how. The conventional picture is that tens of thousands of slaves dragged stones on sledges. But there is no evidence to back this up. Now a Californian software consultant called Maureen Clemmons has suggested that kites might have been involved. While perusing a book on the monuments of Egypt, she noticed a hieroglyph that showed a row of men standing in odd postures. They were holding what looked like ropes that led, via some kind of mechanical system, to a giant bird in the sky. She wondered if perhaps the bird was actually a giant kite, and the men were using it to lift a heavy object.

Intrigued, Clemmons contacted Morteza Gharib, aeronautics professor at the California Institute of Technology. He was fascinated by the idea. 'Coming from Iran, I have a keen interest in Middle Eastern science,' he says. He too was puzzled by the picture that had sparked Clemmons's interest. The object in the sky apparently had wings far too short and wide for a bird. 'The possibility certainly existed that it was a kite,' he says. And since he needed a summer project for his student Emilio Graff, investigating the possibility of using kites as heavy lifters seemed like a good idea.

Gharib and Graff set themselves the task of raising a 4.5-metre stone column from horizontal to vertical, using no source of energy except the wind. Their initial calculations and scale-model wind-tunnel experiments convinced them they wouldn't need a strong wind to lift the 33.5-tonne column. Even a modest force, if sustained over a long time, would do. The key was to use a pulley system that would magnify the applied force. So they rigged up a tent-shaped scaffold directly above the tip of the horizontal column, with pulleys suspended from the scaffold's apex. The idea was that as one end of the column rose, the base would roll across the ground on a trolley.

Earlier this year, the team put Clemmons's unlikely theory to the test, using a 40-square-metre rectangular nylon sail. The kite lifted the column clean off the ground. 'We were absolutely stunned,' Gharib says. 'The instant the sail opened into the wind, a huge force was generated and the column was raised to the vertical in a mere 40 seconds.'

The wind was blowing at a gentle 16 to 20 kilometres an hour, little more than half what they thought would be needed. What they had failed to reckon with was what happened when the kite was opened. 'There was a huge initial force – five times larger than the steady state force,' Gharib says. This jerk meant that kites could lift huge weights, Gharib realised. Even a 300-tonne column could have been lifted to the vertical with 40 or so men and four or five sails. So Clemmons was right: the pyramid builders could have used kites to lift massive stones into place. 'Whether they actually did is another matter,' Gharib says. There are no pictures showing the construction of the pyramids, so there is no way to tell what really happened. 'The evidence for using kites to move large stones is no better or worse than the evidence for the brute force method,' Gharib says.

Indeed, the experiments have left many specialists unconvinced. 'The evidence for kite-lifting is non-existent,' says Willeke Wendrich, an associate professor of Egyptology at the University of California, Los Angeles.

Others feel there is more of a case for the theory. Harnessing the wind would not have been a problem for accomplished sailors like the Egyptians. And they are known to have used wooden pulleys, which could have been made strong enough to bear the weight of massive blocks of stone. In addition, there is some physical evidence that the ancient Egyptians were interested in flight. A wooden artefact found on the step pyramid at Saqqara looks uncannily like a modern glider. Although it dates from several hundred years after the building of the pyramids, its sophistication suggests that the Egyptians might have been developing ideas of flight for a long time. And other ancient civilisations certainly knew about kites; as early as 1250 BC, the Chinese were using them to deliver messages and dump flaming debris on their foes.

The experiments might even have practical uses nowadays. There are plenty of places around the globe where people have no access to heavy machinery, but do know how to deal with wind, sailing and basic mechanical principles. Gharib has already been contacted by a civil engineer in Nicaragua, who wants to put up buildings with adobe roofs supported by concrete arches on a site that heavy equipment can't reach. His idea is to build the arches horizontally, then lift them into place using kites. 'We've given him some design hints,' says Gharib. 'We're just waiting for him to report back.' So whether they were actually used to build the pyramids or not, it seems that kites may make sensible construction tools in the 21st century AD.

Questions 1–7

Do the following statements agree with the information given in Reading Passage 1?

In boxes 1–7 on your answer sheet, write

TRUE	*if the statement agrees with the information*
FALSE	*if the statement contradicts the information*
NOT GIVEN	*if there is no information on this*

1 It is generally believed that large numbers of people were needed to build the pyramids.

2 Clemmons found a strange hieroglyph on the wall of an Egyptian monument.

3 Gharib had previously done experiments on bird flight.

4 Gharib and Graff tested their theory before applying it.

5 The success of the actual experiment was due to the high speed of the wind.

6 They found that, as the kite flew higher, the wind force got stronger.

7 The team decided that it was possible to use kites to raise very heavy stones.

Questions 8–13

Complete the summary below.

*Choose **NO MORE THAN TWO WORDS** from the passage for each answer.*

Write your answers in boxes 8–13 on your answer sheet.

Additional evidence for theory of kite-lifting

The Egyptians had **8** .... , which could lift large pieces of **9** .... , and they knew how to use the energy of the wind from their skill as **10** .... The discovery on one pyramid of an object which resembled a **11** .... suggests they may have experimented with **12** .... In addition, over two thousand years ago kites were used in China as weapons, as well as for sending **13** ....

READING PASSAGE 2

*You should spend about 20 minutes on **Questions 14–26**, which are based on Reading Passage 2 below.*

Endless Harvest

More than two hundred years ago, Russian explorers and fur hunters landed on the Aleutian Islands, a volcanic archipelago in the North Pacific, and learned of a land mass that lay farther to the north. The islands' native inhabitants called this land mass Aleyska, the 'Great Land'; today, we know it as Alaska.

The forty-ninth state to join the United States of America (in 1959), Alaska is fully one-fifth the size of the mainland 48 states combined. It shares, with Canada, the second longest river system in North America and has over half the coastline of the United States. The rivers feed into the Bering Sea and Gulf of Alaska – cold, nutrient-rich waters which support tens of millions of seabirds, and over 400 species of fish, shellfish, crustaceans, and molluscs. Taking advantage of this rich bounty, Alaska's commercial fisheries have developed into some of the largest in the world.

According to the Alaska Department of Fish and Game (ADF&G), Alaska's commercial fisheries landed hundreds of thousands of tonnes of shellfish and herring, and well over a million tonnes of groundfish (cod, sole, perch and pollock) in 2000. The true cultural heart and soul of Alaska's fisheries, however, is salmon. 'Salmon,' notes writer Susan Ewing in The Great Alaska Nature Factbook, 'pump through Alaska like blood through a heart, bringing rhythmic, circulating nourishment to land, animals and people.' The 'predictable abundance of salmon allowed some native cultures to flourish,' and 'dying spawners* feed bears, eagles, other animals, and ultimately the soil itself.' All five species of Pacific salmon – chinook, or king; chum, or dog; coho, or silver; sockeye, or red; and pink, or humpback – spawn** in Alaskan waters, and 90% of all Pacific salmon commercially caught in North America are produced there. Indeed, if Alaska was an independent nation, it would be the largest producer of wild salmon in the world. During 2000, commercial catches of Pacific salmon in Alaska exceeded 320,000 tonnes, with an ex-vessel value of over $US260 million.

Catches have not always been so healthy. Between 1940 and 1959, overfishing led to crashes in salmon populations so severe that in 1953 Alaska was declared a federal disaster area. With the onset of statehood, however, the State of Alaska took over management of its own fisheries, guided by a state constitution which mandates that Alaska's natural resources be managed on a sustainable basis. At that time, statewide harvests totalled around 25 million salmon. Over the next few decades average catches steadily increased as a result of this policy of sustainable

---

* spawners: fish that have released eggs
** spawn: release eggs

management, until, during the 1990s, annual harvests were well in excess of 100 million, and on several occasions over 200 million fish.

The primary reason for such increases is what is known as 'In-Season Abundance-Based Management'. There are biologists throughout the state constantly monitoring adult fish as they show up to spawn. The biologists sit in streamside counting towers, study sonar, watch from aeroplanes, and talk to fishermen. The salmon season in Alaska is not pre-set. The fishermen know the approximate time of year when they will be allowed to fish, but on any given day, one or more field biologists in a particular area can put a halt to fishing. Even sport fishing can be brought to a halt. It is this management mechanism that has allowed Alaska salmon stocks – and, accordingly, Alaska salmon fisheries – to prosper, even as salmon populations in the rest of the United States are increasingly considered threatened or even endangered.

In 1999, the Marine Stewardship Council (MSC)*** commissioned a review of the Alaska salmon fishery. The Council, which was founded in 1996, certifies fisheries that meet high environmental standards, enabling them to use a label that recognises their environmental responsibility. The MSC has established a set of criteria by which commercial fisheries can be judged. Recognising the potential benefits of being identified as environmentally responsible, fisheries approach the Council requesting to undergo the certification process. The MSC then appoints a certification committee, composed of a panel of fisheries experts, which gathers information and opinions from fishermen, biologists, government officials, industry representatives, non-governmental organisations and others.

Some observers thought the Alaska salmon fisheries would not have any chance of certification when, in the months leading up to MSC's final decision, salmon runs throughout western Alaska completely collapsed. In the Yukon and Kuskokwim rivers, chinook and chum runs were probably the poorest since statehood; subsistence communities throughout the region, who normally have priority over commercial fishing, were devastated.

The crisis was completely unexpected, but researchers believe it had nothing to do with impacts of fisheries. Rather, they contend, it was almost certainly the result of climatic shifts, prompted in part by cumulative effects of the el niño/la niña phenomenon on Pacific Ocean temperatures, culminating in a harsh winter in which huge numbers of salmon eggs were frozen. It could have meant the end as far as the certification process was concerned. However, the state reacted quickly, closing down all fisheries, even those necessary for subsistence purposes.

In September 2000, MSC announced that the Alaska salmon fisheries qualified for certification. Seven companies producing Alaska salmon were immediately granted permission to display the MSC logo on their products. Certification is for an initial period of five years, with an annual review to ensure that the fishery is continuing to meet the required standards.

*** MSC: a joint venture between WWF (World Wildlife Fund) and Unilever, a Dutch-based multi-national

Questions 14–20

Do the following statements agree with the information given in Reading Passage 2?

In boxes 14–20 on your answer sheet, write

>   **TRUE**   *if the statement agrees with the information*
>   **FALSE**   *if the statement contradicts the information*
>   **NOT GIVEN**   *if there is no information on this*

14   The inhabitants of the Aleutian islands renamed their islands 'Aleyska'.

15   Alaska's fisheries are owned by some of the world's largest companies.

16   Life in Alaska is dependent on salmon.

17   Ninety per cent of all Pacific salmon caught are sockeye or pink salmon.

18   More than 320,000 tonnes of salmon were caught in Alaska in 2000.

19   Between 1940 and 1959, there was a sharp decrease in Alaska's salmon population.

20   During the 1990s, the average number of salmon caught each year was 100 million.

Questions 21–26

*Complete each sentence with the correct ending, **A–K**, below.*

*Write the correct letter, **A–K**, in boxes 21–26 on your answer sheet.*

21 In Alaska, biologists keep a check on adult fish

22 Biologists have the authority

23 In-Season Abundance-Based Management has allowed the Alaska salmon fisheries

24 The Marine Stewardship Council (MSC) was established

25 As a result of the collapse of the salmon runs in 1999, the state decided

26 In September 2000, the MSC allowed seven Alaska salmon companies

A	to recognise fisheries that care for the environment.
B	to be successful.
C	to stop fish from spawning.
D	to set up environmental protection laws.
E	to stop people fishing for sport.
F	to label their products using the MSC logo.
G	to ensure that fish numbers are sufficient to permit fishing.
H	to assist the subsistence communities in the region.
I	to freeze a huge number of salmon eggs.
J	to deny certification to the Alaska fisheries.
K	to close down all fisheries.

READING PASSAGE 3

*You should spend about 20 minutes on **Questions 27–40**, which are based on Reading Passage 3 below.*

EFFECTS OF NOISE

In general, it is plausible to suppose that we should prefer peace and quiet to noise. And yet most of us have had the experience of having to adjust to sleeping in the mountains or the countryside because it was initially 'too quiet', an experience that suggests that humans are capable of adapting to a wide range of noise levels. Research supports this view. For example, Glass and Singer (1972) exposed people to short bursts of very loud noise and then measured their ability to work out problems and their physiological reactions to the noise. The noise was quite disruptive at first, but after about four minutes the subjects were doing just as well on their tasks as control subjects who were not exposed to noise. Their physiological arousal also declined quickly to the same levels as those of the control subjects.

But there are limits to adaptation and loud noise becomes more troublesome if the person is required to concentrate on more than one task. For example, high noise levels interfered with the performance of subjects who were required to monitor three dials at a time, a task not unlike that of an aeroplane pilot or an air-traffic controller (Broadbent, 1957). Similarly, noise did not affect a subject's ability to track a moving line with a steering wheel, but it did interfere with the subject's ability to repeat numbers while tracking (Finkelman and Glass, 1970).

Probably the most significant finding from research on noise is that its predictability is more important than how loud it is. We are much more able to 'tune out' chronic background noise, even if it is quite loud, than to work under circumstances with unexpected intrusions of noise. In the Glass and Singer study, in which subjects were exposed to bursts of noise as they worked on a task, some subjects heard loud bursts and others heard soft bursts. For some subjects, the bursts were spaced exactly one minute apart (predictable noise); others heard the same amount of noise overall, but the bursts

	Unpredictable Noise	Predictable Noise	Average
Loud noise	40.1	31.8	35.9
Soft noise	36.7	27.4	32.1
Average	38.4	29.6	

Table 1: *Proofreading Errors and Noise*

occurred at random intervals (unpredictable noise). Subjects reported finding the predictable and unpredictable noise equally annoying, and all subjects performed at about the same level during the noise portion of the experiment. But the different noise conditions had quite different after-effects when the subjects were required to proofread written material under conditions of no noise. As shown in Table 1 the unpredictable noise produced more errors in the later proofreading task than predictable noise; and soft, unpredictable noise actually produced slightly more errors on this task than the loud, predictable noise.

Apparently, unpredictable noise produces more fatigue than predictable noise, but it takes a while for this fatigue to take its toll on performance.

Predictability is not the only variable that reduces or eliminates the negative effects of noise. Another is control. If the individual knows that he or she can control the noise, this seems to eliminate both its negative effects at the time and its after-effects. This is true even if the individual never actually exercises his or her option to turn the noise off (Glass and Singer, 1972). Just the knowledge that one has control is sufficient.

The studies discussed so far exposed people to noise for only short periods and only transient effects were studied. But the major worry about noisy environments is that living day after day with chronic noise may produce serious, lasting effects. One study, suggesting that this worry is a realistic one, compared elementary school pupils who attended schools near Los Angeles's busiest airport with students who attended schools in quiet neighbourhoods (Cohen et al., 1980). It was found that children from the noisy schools had higher blood pressure and were more easily distracted than those who attended the quiet schools. Moreover, there was no evidence of adaptability to the noise. In fact, the longer the children had attended the noisy schools, the more distractible they became. The effects also seem to be long lasting. A follow-up study showed that children who were moved to less noisy classrooms still showed greater distractibility one year later than students who had always been in the quiet schools (Cohen et al, 1981). It should be noted that the two groups of children had been carefully matched by the investigators so that they were comparable in age, ethnicity, race, and social class.

Questions 27–29

*Choose the correct letter, **A**, **B**, **C** or **D**.*

Write the correct letter in boxes 27–29 on your answer sheet.

27 The writer suggests that people may have difficulty sleeping in the mountains because

    A   humans do not prefer peace and quiet to noise.
    B   they may be exposed to short bursts of very strange sounds.
    C   humans prefer to hear a certain amount of noise while they sleep.
    D   they may have adapted to a higher noise level in the city.

28 In noise experiments, Glass and Singer found that

    A   problem-solving is much easier under quiet conditions.
    B   physiological arousal prevents the ability to work.
    C   bursts of noise do not seriously disrupt problem-solving in the long term.
    D   the physiological arousal of control subjects declined quickly.

29 Researchers discovered that high noise levels are not likely to interfere with the

    A   successful performance of a single task.
    B   tasks of pilots or air traffic controllers.
    C   ability to repeat numbers while tracking moving lines.
    D   ability to monitor three dials at once.

Questions 30–34

*Complete the summary using the list of words and phrases, **A–J**, below.*

*Write the correct letter, **A–J**, in boxes 30–34 on your answer sheet.*

NB   *You may use any letter more than once.*

Glass and Singer (1972) showed that situations in which there is intense noise have less effect on performance than circumstances in which **30** .... noise occurs. Subjects were divided into groups to perform a task. Some heard loud bursts of noise, others soft. For some subjects, the noise was predictable, while for others its occurrence was random. All groups were exposed to **31** .... noise. The predictable noise group **32** .... the unpredictable noise group on this task.

In the second part of the experiment, the four groups were given a proofreading task to complete under conditions of no noise. They were required to check written material for errors. The group which had been exposed to unpredictable noise **33** .... the group which had been exposed to predictable noise. The group which had been exposed to loud predictable noise performed better than those who had heard soft, unpredictable bursts. The results suggest that **34** .... noise produces fatigue but that this manifests itself later.

A	no control over
B	unexpected
C	intense
D	the same amount of
E	performed better than
F	performed at about the same level as
G	no
H	showed more irritation than
I	made more mistakes than
J	different types of

Questions 35–40

Look at the following statements (Questions 35–40) and the list of researchers below.

Match each statement with the correct researcher(s), A–E.

Write the correct letter, A–E, in boxes 35–40 on your answer sheet.

NB   You may use any letter more than once.

35   Subjects exposed to noise find it difficult at first to concentrate on problem-solving tasks.

36   Long-term exposure to noise can produce changes in behaviour which can still be observed a year later.

37   The problems associated with exposure to noise do not arise if the subject knows they can make it stop.

38   Exposure to high-pitched noise results in more errors than exposure to low-pitched noise.

39   Subjects find it difficult to perform three tasks at the same time when exposed to noise.

40   Noise affects a subject's capacity to repeat numbers while carrying out another task.

List of Researchers

A   Glass and Singer
B   Broadbent
C   Finkelman and Glass
D   Cohen et al.
E   None of the above

WRITING

WRITING TASK 1

You should spend about 20 minutes on this task.

> *The pie charts below show units of electricity production by fuel source in Australia and France in 1980 and 2000.*
>
> *Summarise the information by selecting and reporting the main features, and make comparisons where relevant.*

Write at least 150 words.

Units of electricity by fuel source in Australia

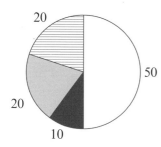

1980
Total Production:
100 units

2000
Total Production:
170 units

Units of electricity by fuel source in France

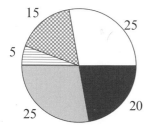

1980
Total Production:
90 units

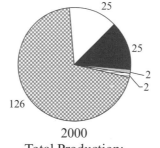
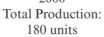

2000
Total Production:
180 units

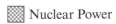 Coal

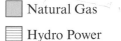 Oil

Natural Gas

Hydro Power

Nuclear Power

WRITING TASK 2

You should spend about 40 minutes on this task.

Write about the following topic:

> *Some people think that universities should provide graduates with the knowledge and skills needed in the workplace. Others think that the true function of a university should be to give access to knowledge for its own sake, regardless of whether the course is useful to an employer.*
>
> *What, in your opinion, should be the main function of a university?*

Give reasons for your answer and include any relevant examples from your own knowledge or experience.

Write at least 250 words.

SPEAKING

PART 1

The examiner asks the candidate about him/herself, his/her home, work or studies and other familiar topics.

EXAMPLE

Travelling to work or college

- How do you usually travel to work or college? [Why?]
- Have you always travelled to work/college in the same way? [Why/Why not?]
- What do you like about travelling to work/college this way?
- What changes would improve the way you travel to work/college? [Why?]

PART 2

> **Describe a piece of electronic equipment that you find useful.**
>
> **You should say:**
>   what it is
>   how you learned to use it
>   how long you have had it
> **and explain why you find this piece of electronic equipment useful.**

You will have to talk about the topic for one to two minutes.
You have one minute to think about what you are going to say.
You can make some notes to help you if you wish.

PART 3

Discussion topics:

Technology and housework

Example questions:
What kinds of machine are used for housework in modern homes in your country?
How have these machines benefited people? Are there any negative effects of using them?
Do you think all new homes will be equipped with household machines in the future? Why?

Technology in the workplace

Example questions:
What kinds of equipment do most workers need to use in offices today?
How have developments in technology affected employment in your country?
Some people think that technology has brought more stress than benefits to employed people nowadays. Would you agree or disagree? Why?

General Training Reading and Writing Test A

SECTION 1   *Questions 1–14*

Read the text below and answer Questions 1–7.

EASTERN ENERGY

We are here to help and provide you with personal advice on any matters connected with your bill or any other queries regarding your gas and electricity supply.

Moving home
Please give as much notice as possible if you are moving home, but at least 48 hours is required for us to make the necessary arrangements for your gas and electricity supply. Please telephone our 24-hour line on 01316 753219 with details of your move. In most cases we are happy to accept your meter reading on the day you move. Tell the new occupant that Eastern Energy supply the household, to ensure the service is not interrupted. Remember we can now supply electricity and gas at your new address, anywhere in the UK. If you do not contact us, you may be held responsible for the payment for electricity used after you have moved.

Meter reading
Eastern Energy uses various types of meter ranging from the traditional dial meter to new technology digital display meters. Always read the meter from left to right, ignoring any red dials. If you require assistance, contact our 24-hour line on 0600 7310 310.

Energy Efficiency Line
If you would like advice on the efficient use of energy, please call our Energy Efficiency Line on 0995 7626 513. Please do not use this number for any other enquiries.

Special services
Passwords – you can choose a password so that, whenever we visit you at home, you will know it is us. For more information, ring our helpline on 0995 7290 290.

Help and advice
If you need help or advice with any issues, please contact us on 01316 440188.

Complaints
We hope you will never have a problem or cause to complain, but, if you do, please contact our complaints handling team at PO Box 220, Stanfield, ST55 6GF or telephone us on 01316 753270.

Supply failure
If you experience any problems with your electricity supply, please call free on 0600 7838 836, 24 hours a day, seven days a week.

Questions 1–7

Do the following statements agree with the information given in the text on page 104?

In boxes 1–7 on your answer sheet, write

>**TRUE**   *if the statement agrees with the information*
>**FALSE**   *if the statement contradicts the information*
>**NOT GIVEN** *if there is no information on this*

1   Customers should inform Eastern Energy of a change of address on arrival at their new home.

2   Customers are expected to read their own gas or electricity meters.

3   It is now cheaper to use gas rather than electricity as a form of heating.

4   Eastern Energy supplies energy to households throughout the country.

5   The Energy Efficiency Line also handles queries about energy supply.

6   All complaints about energy supply should be made by phone.

7   Customers are not charged for the call when they report a fault in supply.

Questions 8–14

The text on page 107 has seven sections, **A–G.**

Choose the correct heading for each section from the list of headings below.

*Write the correct number, **i–x**, in boxes 8–14 on your answer sheet.*

List of Headings
i   Re-heating
ii   Foods with skins
iii   Keeping your oven clean
iv   Standing time
v   Rapid cooking times
vi   Using a thermometer
vii   Small quantities of food
viii Deep fat frying
ix   Foods low in moisture
x   Liquids

8   Section **A**

9   Section **B**

10   Section **C**

11   Section **D**

12   Section **E**

13   Section **F**

14   Section **G**

Using your new microwave oven

Some important points to note

A   As microwave cooking times are much shorter than other cooking times, it is essential that recommended cooking times are not exceeded without first checking the food.

B   Take care when heating small amounts of food as these can easily burn, dry out or catch fire if cooked too long. Always set short cooking times and check the food frequently.

C   Take care when heating 'dry' foods, e.g. bread items, chocolate and pastries. These can easily burn or catch fire if cooked too long.

D   Some processed meats, such as sausages, have non-porous casings. These must be pierced by a fork before cooking, to prevent bursting. Whole fruit and vegetables should be similarly treated.

E   When heating soup, sauces and beverages in your microwave oven, heating beyond boiling point can occur without evidence of bubbling. Care should be taken not to overheat.

F   When warming up food for a second time, it is essential that it is served 'piping hot', i.e. steam is being emitted from all parts and any sauce is bubbling. For foods that cannot be stirred, e.g. pizza, the centre should be cut with a knife to test it is well heated through.

G   It is important for the safe operation of the oven that it is wiped out regularly. Use warm, soapy water, squeeze the cloth out well and use it to remove any grease or food from the interior. The oven should be unplugged during this process.

SECTION 2   *Questions 15–27*

Read the text below and answer Questions 15–20.

CHOOSING PREMISES FOR A NEW BUSINESS

What you need

Three factors dominate the priorities of small businesses looking for premises: cost, cost and cost. Nobody ever has enough money, so there is an overwhelming temptation to go for the cheapest property. It is a mistake that can take decades to rectify – and even threaten the future of a promising business.

Ironically some firms swing too far in the other direction, committing themselves to a heavy initial outlay because they believe in the importance of image – and that does not come cheap. Finding the right premises is the real secret. That can, and will, vary enormously according to the type of business. But there are some general rules that apply to any operation.

Location

High street premises are important for shops which rely on passing trade – but these are expensive. Rents fall quickly within a few metres of main roads. Offices, however, need not be located centrally, particularly if most business is done on the phone or via email.

Manufacturing and storage relies heavily on access. Think about how vans and lorries will deliver and collect goods from the premises. Nearby parking can be important for staff, and public transport can be even more so, as traffic restrictions tighten.

Size

This is a crucial decision. Health and Safety laws provide basic guidance on how much room is required per office desk or manufacturing operation. But remember to allow for growth.

Growth

Every small business aims to become a big business, but this prospect can be obstructed if the wrong decisions are made early on. It is important to consider flexibility from the start. Can a building be physically altered internally by knocking down walls or by extending outwards or adding extra floors? Is there spare land next door to expand later if necessary?

Landlords obviously have to agree to any changes so it is important that the contract includes details of what will be allowed and how much extra will be charged on top of the costs of rebuilding or alteration. Planning rules must also be considered. Local authorities are not always open to discussion about the future of premises. They may have rigid rules about increasing density of development. The building may be in a conservation area or near housing, in which case it will be much more difficult to consider changes.

Questions 15–20

Complete the sentences below.

*Choose **NO MORE THAN TWO WORDS** from the text for each answer.*

Write your answers in boxes 15–20 on your answer sheet.

15 Some people choose expensive premises because they want to create an impressive .... for their company.

16 Businesses which depend on .... need to be on or near the principal shopping areas.

17 Businesses which produce goods must check there is .... to the premises for delivery vehicles.

18 When choosing a building for your premises, find out whether .... could be removed to create more room.

19 Make sure that the .... states what type of building alterations might be permitted.

20 If business premises are located close to .... , extensions may not be allowed.

Read the text below and answer Questions 21–27.

CALIFORNIA STATE COLLEGE

WORKING CONDITIONS AND BENEFITS FOR EMPLOYEES

Payday

Employees are paid every other Friday. If Friday is a holiday, payday will be the following Monday. Generally, employees pick up the pay checks in their department; if not, they may be picked up at the Business Office.

Overtime

All time worked over eight hours in one day and forty hours in a workweek, and also the first eight hours worked on the seventh day of work in a workweek is considered overtime for non-exempt employees. The supervisor must approve all overtime before overtime occurs. Hours in excess of eight hours on the seventh day and in excess of twelve hours in one day will be paid at double time. Exempt employees receive no additional compensation for overtime hours.

Parking

All employees who will be parking in a staff parking zone must obtain a parking permit. A monthly pre-tax payroll deduction can be made by visiting Human Resources. If you wish to pay cash, present your staff I.D. and license number to the Cashier's Office. The Safety Department will ticket cars without a parking permit and a fine will be applied.

I.D. Card

All employees are required to carry an I.D. card. If an employee loses his/her card, there will be an automatic charge of $5.00 to issue a duplicate. If an employee gives up employment, his/her I.D. card must be returned prior to release of final paycheck.

Holidays

All regular and temporary full-time employees generally receive approximately 13 paid holidays during the course of each calendar year. Regular part-time employees will receive holiday benefits worked out using a prorated system. The holiday schedule is initiated annually.

Personal Holiday

Each employee is granted one extra day as a Personal Holiday at the time of hire, and at the beginning of each calendar year. Personal Holiday hours must be taken at one time (eight hours full-time or prorated based on the employee's time). Employees requesting Personal Holiday will be required to complete 'Leave Request' forms. No more than one Personal Holiday is authorized annually.

Birthday Holiday

All regular and temporary full-time or part-time employees are entitled to take their birthday off with pay. An employee has a fifteen-day span before and following his/her birthday to take the paid day off. What is known as a grace period through January 15th is given to those employees whose birthdays fall between December 16th and the end of the year.

Questions 21–27

Answer the questions below.

*Choose **NO MORE THAN THREE WORDS** from the text for each answer.*

Write your answers in boxes 21–27 on your answer sheet.

21   Where do most employees collect their wages?

22   Who has to authorise any overtime an employee wishes to do?

23   Who is not paid extra for working more than 40 hours a week?

24   Where should employees go if they wish to have the parking charge taken off their salary?

25   What method is used to calculate part-time employees' holidays?

26   Which documents must employees fill in to select their Personal Holiday?

27   What is the name of the special entitlement provided to employees with birthdays in the second half of December?

SECTION 3   *Questions 28–40*

Read the text on pages 112 and 113 and answer Questions 28–40.

A Very Special Dog

Florence is one of a new breed of dog who is making the work of the Australian Customs much easier.

It is 8.15 a.m. A flight lands at Melbourne's Tullamarine International Airport. Several hundred pieces of baggage are rushed from the plane onto a conveyor belt in the baggage reclaim annexe. Over the sound of roaring engines, rushing air vents and grinding generators, a dog barks. Florence, a sleek black labrador, wags her tail.

Among the cavalcade of luggage passing beneath Florence's all-smelling nose, is a nondescript hardback suitcase. Inside the case, within styrofoam casing, packed in loose pepper and coffee, wrapped in freezer paper and heat-sealed in plastic, are 18 kilograms of hashish.

The cleverly concealed drugs don't fool super-sniffer Florence, and her persistent scratching at the case alerts her handler. Florence is one of a truly new breed: the product of what is perhaps the only project in the world dedicated to breeding dogs solely to detect drugs. Ordinary dogs have a 0.1% chance of making it in drug detection. The new breeding programme, run by the Australian Customs, is so successful that more than 50% of its dogs make the grade.

And what began as a wholly practical exercise in keeping illegal drugs out of Australia may end up playing a role in an entirely different sphere – the comparatively esoteric world of neurobiology. It turns out that it's not Florence's nose that makes her a top drug dog, but her unswerving concentration, plus a few other essential traits. Florence could help neurobiologists to understand both what they call 'attention processing', the brain mechanisms that determine what a person pays attention to and for how long, and its flip side, problems such as Attention Deficit/Hyperactivity Disorder (ADHD). As many as 3 to 5% of children are thought to suffer from the condition in the US, where the incidence is highest, although diagnosis is often controversial.

The Australian Customs has used dogs to find drugs since 1969. Traditionally, the animals came from pounds and private breeders. But, in 1993, fed up with the poor success rate of finding good dogs this way, John Vandeloo, senior instructor with the Detector Dog Unit, joined forces with Kath Champness, then a doctoral student at the University of Melbourne, and set up a breeding programme.

Champness began by defining six essential traits that make a detector dog. First, every good detector dog must love praise because this is the only tool trainers have at their disposal, but the dog must still be able to work for long periods without it. Then it needs a strong hunting instinct and the stamina to keep sniffing at the taxing rate of around 300 times per minute. The ideal detector is also fearless enough to deal with jam-packed airport crowds and the roaring engine rooms of cargo ships.

The remaining two traits are closely related and cognitive in nature. A good detector must be capable of focusing on the task of searching for drugs, despite the distractions in any airport or dockside. This is what neurobiologists call 'selective attention'. And finally, with potentially tens of thousands of hiding places for drugs, the dog must persevere and maintain focus for hours at a time. Neurobiologists call this 'sustained attention'.

Vandeloo and Champness assess the dogs' abilities to concentrate by marking them on a scale of between one and five according to how well they remain focused on a toy tossed into a patch of grass. Ivan scores a feeble one. He follows the toy, gets half-way there, then becomes distracted by places where the other dogs have been or by flowers in the paddock. Rowena, on the other hand, has phenomenal concentration; some might even consider her obsessive. When Vandeloo tosses the toy, nothing can distract her from the searching, not other dogs, not food. And even if no one is around to encourage her, she keeps looking just the same. Rowena gets a five.

A person's ability to pay attention, like a dog's, depends on a number of overlapping cognitive behaviours, including memory and learning – the neurobiologist's attention processing. Attention in humans can be tested by asking subjects to spot colours on a screen while ignoring shapes, or to spot sounds while ignoring visual cues, or to take a 'vigilance test'. Sitting a vigilance test is like being a military radar operator. Blips appear on a cluttered monitor infrequently and at irregular intervals. Rapid detection of all blips earns a high score. Five minutes into the test, one in ten subjects will start to miss the majority of the blips, one in ten will still be able to spot nearly all of them and the rest will come somewhere in between.

Vigilance tasks provide signals that are infrequent and unpredictable – which is exactly what is expected of the dogs when they are asked to notice just a few odour molecules in the air, and then to home in on the source. During a routine mail screen that can take hours, the dogs stay so focused that not even a postcard lined with 0.5 grams of heroin and hidden in a bulging sack of letters escapes detection.

With the current interest in attentional processing, as well as human conditions that have an attention deficit component, such as ADHD, it is predicted that it is only a matter of time before the super-sniffer dogs attract the attention of neurobiologists trying to cure these conditions.

Questions 28–32

*Choose the correct letter, **A**, **B**, **C** or **D**.*

Write the correct letter in boxes 28–32 on your answer sheet.

28 The drugs in the suitcase

    A were hidden inside the lining.
    B had pepper and coffee around them.
    C had previously been frozen.
    D had a special smell to repel dogs.

29 Most dogs are not good at finding drugs because

    A they don't work well with a handler.
    B they lack the right training.
    C the drugs are usually very well hidden.
    D they lack certain genetic qualities.

30 Florence is a good drug detector because she

    A has a better sense of smell than other dogs.
    B is not easily distracted.
    C has been specially trained to work at airports.
    D enjoys what she is doing.

31 Dogs like Florence may help scientists understand

    A how human and dog brains differ.
    B how people can use both sides of their brain.
    C why some people have difficulty paying attention.
    D the best way for people to maintain their focus.

32 In 1993, the Australian Customs

    A decided to use its own dogs again.
    B was successful in finding detector dogs.
    C changed the way it obtained dogs.
    D asked private breeders to provide more dogs.

Questions 33–36

*Choose **FOUR** letters, A–J.*

Write the correct letters in boxes 33–36 on your answer sheet.

The writer mentions a number of important qualities that detector dogs must have.

Which **FOUR** of the following qualities are mentioned by the writer of the text?

    A   a good relationship with people
    B   a willingness to work in smelly conditions
    C   quick reflexes
    D   an ability to work in noisy conditions
    E   an ability to maintain concentration
    F   a willingness to work without constant encouragement
    G   the skill to find things in long grass
    H   experience as hunters
    I   a desire for people's approval
    J   the ability to search a large number of places rapidly

Questions 37–40

Do the following statements agree with the information given in the text?

In boxes 37–40 on your answer sheet, write

TRUE	*if the statement agrees with the information*
FALSE	*if the statement contradicts the information*
NOT GIVEN	*if there is no information on this*

37   Methods of determining if a child has ADHD are now widely accepted.

38   After about five minutes of a vigilance test, some subjects will still notice some blips.

39   Vigilance tests help improve concentration.

40   If a few grams of a drug are well concealed, even the best dogs will miss them.

WRITING

WRITING TASK 1

You should spend about 20 minutes on this task.

You have recently started work in a new company.

Write a letter to an English-speaking friend. In your letter

- *explain why you changed jobs*
- *describe your new job*
- *tell him/her your other news*

Write at least 150 words.

You do NOT need to write any addresses.

Begin your letter as follows:

Dear .... ,

WRITING TASK 2

You should spend about 40 minutes on this task.

Write about the following topic:

Some people prefer to live in a house, while others feel that there are more advantages to living in an apartment.

Are there more advantages than disadvantages of living in a house compared with living in an apartment?

Give reasons for your answer and include any relevant examples from your own knowledge or experience.

Write at least 250 words.

General Training Reading and Writing Test B

SECTION 1   *Questions 1–14*

Read the text below and answer Questions 1–7.

CALL ANYWHERE IN THE STATE FOR ONE LOW SHORT-DISTANCE RATE!

You have a choice of three Supafone Mobile Digital access plans: Leisuretime, Executive and Highflier. They are designed to meet the needs of light, moderate and high-volume users. Calls in each plan are charged at only two rates – short-distance and long-distance. You enjoy big savings with off-peak calls.

LEISURETIME
Your mobile phone is mainly for personal use. You use your phone to keep family and friends in touch. You don't want to strain your budget.
With this plan you enjoy the lowest monthly access fee and extremely competitive costs for calls. However, a monthly minimum call charge applies.

EXECUTIVE
You're in business and need to be able to call your office and your clients whenever the need arises. You value the convenience of a mobile phone but need to keep a close eye on overheads.
For frequent users: the monthly access fee is slightly higher, but you enjoy the savings of a discounted call rate.

HIGHFLIER
You are always on the move and communications are critical. You need to be able to call and be called wherever you are – world-wide.
As a high-volume user you pay an access fee of just $60 a month but even lower call rates.

	LEISURETIME		EXECUTIVE		HIGHFLIER	
Monthly Access Fee	$35		$46		$60	
	PEAK 30 sec. unit	OFF PEAK Save 50%	PEAK 30 sec. unit	OFF PEAK Save 50%	PEAK 30 sec. unit	OFF PEAK Save 50%
Short-distance	21.0 cents	10.5 cents	16.8 cents	8.4 cents	15.1 cents	7.6 cents
Long-distance	31.5 cents	16.8 cents	25.2 cents	12.6 cents	21.0 cents	11.4 cents
Best if you spend this amount a month on calls	up to $95		$95 – $180		more than $180	

Peak time: 7 a.m. to 7 p.m. Monday-Saturday

Off peak: all other times, including all day Sunday. Billing increments are in 30-second units. Call charges are rounded up to the nearest cent. In off-peak periods, calls are subject to a minimum charge of two 30-second units.

Once-only Connection Fee: $30 plus additional $35 for your SmartCard.

Questions 1–7

Classify the following statements as referring to

> **A**   the LEISURETIME plan
> **B**   the EXECUTIVE plan
> **C**   the HIGHFLIER plan
> **D**   ALL three of the plans

*Write the correct letter, **A**, **B**, **C** or **D**, in boxes 1–7 on your answer sheet.*

1   The monthly access fee is the highest but the call rates are the lowest.

2   Calls are charged at short-distance or long-distance rates.

3   This plan is **NOT** primarily intended for people who need a mobile phone for their work.

4   This plan is a cost-effective choice if you spend just over $100 a month on calls.

5   It costs 21 cents for a 30-second long-distance call at 2 p.m.

6   The connection fee is $30.

7   You will have to pay a minimum amount for calls each month.

Read the text below and answer Questions 8–14.

Westwinds Farm Campsite

Open April – September
(Booking is advised for holidays in July and August to guarantee a place.)

Jim and Meg Oaks welcome you to the campsite. We hope you will enjoy your stay here.

We ask all campers to show due care and consideration whilst staying here and to observe the following camp rules.

- **Keep the campsite clean and tidy:**

  – dispose of litter in the bins provided;
  – leave the showers, toilets and washing area in the same state as you found them;
  – ensure your site is clear of all litter when you leave it.

- **Don't obstruct rights of way.** Keep cars, bikes, etc. off the road.

- **Let sleeping campers have some peace.** Don't make any noise after 10 o'clock at night or before 7.30 in the morning.

- **Dogs must be kept on a lead.** Owners of dogs that disturb other campers by barking through the night will be asked to leave.

- **Disorderly behaviour will not be tolerated.**

- **The lighting of fires is strictly prohibited.**

- **Ball games are not allowed on the campsite.** There is plenty of room for ball games in the park opposite the campsite.

- **Radios, portable music equipment, etc. must not be played at high volume.**

The management reserves the right to refuse admittance.

Questions 8–14

Do the following statements agree with the information given in the text on page 119?

In boxes 8–14 on your answer sheet, write

>**TRUE**   *if the statement agrees with the information*
>**FALSE**   *if the statement contradicts the information*
>**NOT GIVEN**   *if there is no information on this*

8   The campsite is open all year round.

9   You should book ahead for the busier times of the year.

10   The minimum stay at the campsite is two nights.

11   The entrance to the campsite is locked after 10 p.m.

12   No dogs are allowed on the campsite.

13   You are not allowed to cook food on open fires.

14   The owners of the campsite may not allow you to camp there.

SECTION 2   *Questions 15–27*

Read the text below and answer Questions 15–27.

The law on minimum pay

Who is entitled to minimum pay?

Nearly all workers aged 16 years and over, including part-time workers, are entitled to the National Minimum Wage. Amongst those to whom it does **not** apply are those engaged in unpaid work and family members employed by the family business.

What is the minimum wage that I am entitled to?

The National Wage Act specifies the minimum rates of pay applicable nationwide. Since 1 October 2007, the adult rate for workers aged 22 and over has been £5.25 per hour. The development rate for 18–21 year olds and for workers getting training in the first 6 months of a job is £4.60 per hour. The rate for 16–17 year olds starts at £3.40 an hour. There are special provisions for some workers, for example those whose job includes accommodation. Pay means gross pay and includes any items paid through the payroll such as overtime, bonus payments, commission and tips and gratuities.

I believe I'm being paid below the National Minimum Wage Rate. How can I complain?

If you are being paid less than this, there are various steps you can take:

- If you feel able, you should talk directly with your employer. This is a clear legal right, and employers can be fined for not paying the NMW.
- If you are a trade union member, you should call in the union.
- If neither of these is appropriate then you can email via the Revenue and Customs website or call their helpline for advice.

You have the legal right to inspect your employer's pay records if you believe, on reasonable grounds, that you are being paid less than the NMW. Your employer is required to produce the records within 14 days, and must make them available at your place of work or at some other reasonable place. If your employer fails to produce the records, you may take the matter to an employment tribunal. You must make your complaint within three months of the ending of the 14-day notice period.

Questions 15–21

Complete the sentences below.

*Choose **NO MORE THAN TWO WORDS AND/OR A NUMBER** from the text for each answer.*

Write your answers in boxes 15–21 on your answer sheet.

15 The law on minimum pay doesn't cover you if you are working in your .... or if you are a volunteer.

16 You may be paid under £5 an hour if you are receiving .... at the start of a job.

17 There are different rules for people who are provided with .... with their jobs.

18 If you earn extra money, for example for working longer hours or in tips, this counts as part of your wage when you receive it via ....

19 Anyone being paid below the National Minimum Wage should speak to their .... if they can.

20 According to the law, you can ask to look at your boss's ....

21 You have a period of .... to complain if your boss does not co-operate within the specified period of time.

Read the text below and answer Questions 22–27.

Dealing with your office emails

Email has completely changed the way we work today. It offers many benefits and, if used well, can be an excellent tool for improving your own efficiency. Managed badly, though, email can be a waste of valuable time. Statistics indicate that office workers need to wade through an average of more than 30 emails a day. Despite your best efforts, unsolicited email or spam can clutter up the most organised inbox and infect your computer system with viruses. Here we give you guidance on protecting yourself.

Prioritising incoming messages

If you are regularly faced with a large volume of incoming messages, you need to prioritise your inbox to identify which emails are really important. If it is obvious spam, it can be deleted without reading. Then follow these steps for each email:

- Check who the email is from. Were you expecting or hoping to hear from the sender? How quickly do they expect you to respond?
- Check what the email is about. Is the subject urgent? Is it about an issue that falls within your sphere of responsibility, or should it just be forwarded to someone else?
- Has the email been in your inbox for long? Check the message time.

An initial scan like this can help you identify the emails that require your prompt attention. The others can be kept for reading at a more convenient time.

Replying in stages

Having prioritised your emails, you can answer them in stages, first with a brief acknowledgement and then a more detailed follow-up. This is particularly advisable when dealing with complicated matters where you don't want to give a rushed answer. If you decide to do this, tell the recipient a definite date when you'll be able to get back to him or her and try to keep to this wherever possible.

Some emails are uncomplicated and only require a brief, one line answer, so it's a good idea to reply to these immediately. For example, if all you need to say is, 'Yes, I can make the 10.00 meeting', or 'Thanks, that's just the information I needed', do it. If you are unable to reply there and then or choose not to, let the sender know that you've received the message and will be in touch as soon as possible.

Questions 22–27

Complete the flow chart below.

*Choose **NO MORE THAN TWO WORDS** from the text for each answer.*

Write your answers in boxes 22–27 on your answer sheet.

Dealing with emails

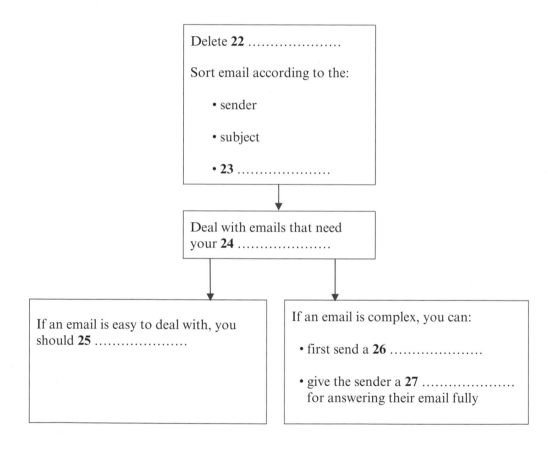

Delete **22** ....

Sort email according to the:

- sender

- subject

- **23** ....

⬇

Deal with emails that need your **24** ....

If an email is easy to deal with, you should **25** ....

If an email is complex, you can:

- first send a **26** ....

- give the sender a **27** .... for answering their email fully

SECTION 3   *Questions 28–40*

Read the text on pages 125 and 126 and answer Questions 28–40.

THE IRON BRIDGE

The Iron Bridge was the first of its kind in Europe and is universally recognised as a symbol of the Industrial Revolution.

A The Iron Bridge crosses the River Severn in Coalbrookdale, in the west of England. It was the first cast-iron bridge to be successfully erected, and the first large cast-iron structure of the industrial age in Europe, although the Chinese were expert iron-casters many centuries earlier.

B Rivers used to be the equivalent of today's motorways, in that they were extensively used for transportation. The River Severn, which starts its life on the Welsh mountains and eventually enters the sea between Cardiff and Bristol, is the longest navigable river in Britain. It was ideal for transportation purposes, and special boats were built to navigate the waters. By the middle of the eighteenth century, the Severn was one of the busiest rivers in Europe. Local goods, including coal, iron products, wool, grain and cider, were sent by river. Among the goods coming upstream were luxuries such as sugar, tea, coffee and wine. In places, the riverbanks were lined with wharves and the river was often crowded with boats loading or unloading.

C In 1638, Basil Brooke patented a steel-making process and built a furnace at Coalbrookdale. This later became the property of Abraham Darby (referred to as Abraham Darby I to distinguish him from his son and grandson of the same name). After serving an apprenticeship in Birmingham, Darby had started a business in Bristol, but he moved to Coalbrookdale in 1710 with an idea that coke derived from coal could provide a more economical alternative to charcoal as a fuel for ironmaking. This led to cheaper, more efficient ironmaking from the abundant supplies of coal, iron and limestone in the area.

D His son, Abraham Darby II, pioneered the manufacture of cast iron, and had the idea of building a bridge over the Severn, as ferrying stores of all kinds across the river, particularly the large quantities of fuel for the furnaces at Coalbrookdale and other surrounding ironworks, involved considerable expense and delay. However, it was his son Abraham Darby III (born in 1750) who, in 1775, organised a meeting to plan the building of a bridge. This was designed by a local architect, Thomas Pritchard, who had the idea of constructing it of iron.

E Sections were cast during the winter of 1778–9 for a 7-metre-wide bridge with a span of 31 metres, 12 metres above the river. Construction took three months during the summer of 1779, and remarkably, nobody was injured during the construction process – a feat almost unheard of even in modern major civil engineering projects. Work on the approach roads continued for another two years, and the bridge was opened to traffic in 1781. Abraham Darby III funded the bridge by commissioning paintings and engravings, but he lost a lot on the project, which had cost nearly double the estimate, and he died leaving massive debts in 1789, aged only 39. The district did not flourish for much longer, and during the nineteenth and early twentieth centuries factories closed down. Since 1934 the bridge has been open only to pedestrians. Universally recognised as the symbol of the Industrial Revolution, the Iron Bridge now stands at the heart of the Ironbridge Gorge World Heritage Site.

F It has always been a mystery how the bridge was built. Despite its pioneering technology, no eye-witness accounts are known which describe the iron bridge being erected – and certainly no plans have survived. However, recent discoveries, research and experiments have shed new light on exactly how it was built, challenging the assumptions of recent decades. In 1997 a small watercolour sketch by Elias Martin came to light in the Swedish capital, Stockholm. Although there is a wealth of early views of the bridge by numerous artists, this is the only one which actually shows it under construction.

G Up until recently it had been assumed that the bridge had been built from both banks, with the inner supports tilted across the river. This would have allowed river traffic to continue unimpeded during construction. But the picture clearly shows sections of the bridge being raised from a barge in the river. It contradicted everything historians had assumed about the bridge, and it was even considered that the picture could have been a fake as no other had come to light. So in 2001 a half-scale model of the bridge was built, in order to see if it could have been constructed in the way depicted in the watercolour. Meanwhile, a detailed archaeological, historical and photographic survey was done by the Ironbridge Gorge Museum Trust, along with a 3D CAD (computer-aided design) model by English Heritage.

H The results tell us a lot more about how the bridge was built. We now know that all the large castings were made individually as they are all slightly different. The bridge wasn't welded or bolted together as metal bridges are these days. Instead it was fitted together using a complex system of joints normally used for wood – but this was the traditional way in which iron structures were joined at the time. The construction of the model proved that the painting shows a very realistic method of constructing the bridge that could work and was in all probability the method used.

I Now only one mystery remains in the Iron Bridge story. The Swedish watercolour sketch had apparently been torn from a book which would have contained similar sketches. It had been drawn by a Swedish artist who lived in London for 12 years and travelled Britain drawing what he saw. Nobody knows what has happened to the rest of the book, but perhaps the other sketches still exist somewhere. If they are ever found they could provide further valuable evidence of how the Iron Bridge was constructed.

Questions 28–31

Answer the questions below.

Choose ONE NUMBER ONLY from the text for each answer.

Write your answers in boxes 28–31 on your answer sheet.

28 When was the furnace bought by Darby originally constructed?

29 When were the roads leading to the bridge completed?

30 When was the bridge closed to traffic?

31 When was a model of the bridge built?

Questions 32–36

Do the following statements agree with the information given in the text?

In boxes 32–36 on your answer sheet, write

TRUE	*if the statement agrees with the information*
FALSE	*if the statement contradicts the information*
NOT GIVEN	*if there is no information on this*

32 There is no written evidence of how the original bridge was constructed.

33 The painting by Elias Martin is the only one of the bridge when it was new.

34 The painting shows that the bridge was constructed from the two banks.

35 The original bridge and the model took equally long to construct.

36 Elias Martin is thought to have made other paintings of the bridge.

Questions 37–40

The text has nine paragraphs, **A–I**.

Which paragraph contains the following information?

*Write the correct letter, **A–I**, in boxes 37–40 on your answer sheet.*

37 why a bridge was required across the River Severn

38 a method used to raise money for the bridge

39 why Coalbrookdale became attractive to iron makers

40 how the sections of the bridge were connected to each other

WRITING

WRITING TASK 1

You should spend about 20 minutes on this task.

---

*Last month you had a holiday overseas where you stayed with some friends.
They have just sent you some photos of your holiday.*

Write a letter to your friends. In your letter

- *thank them for the photos and for the holiday*
- *explain why you didn't write earlier*
- *invite them to come and stay with you*

Write at least 150 words.

You do NOT need to write any addresses.

Begin your letter as follows:

Dear .... ,

WRITING TASK 2

You should spend about 40 minutes on this task.

Write about the following topic:

---

*Some people feel that entertainers (e.g. film stars, pop musicians or sports
stars) are paid too much money.*

Do you agree or disagree?

Which other types of job should be highly paid?

Give reasons for your answer and include any relevant examples from your own knowledge
or experience.

Write at least 250 words.

Tapescripts

TEST 1

SECTION 1

MAN: Hello, this is Land Transport Information at Toronto Airport. How may I help you?

WOMAN: Oh, good morning. Um, I'm flying to Toronto Airport next week, and I need to get to a town called um, Milton. Could you tell me how I can get there?

MAN: Milton, did you say? Let me see. I think that's about 150 miles south-west of here. In fact it's 147 miles to be exact, so it'll take you at least – say, three to four hours by road. *Example*

WOMAN: Wow! Is it as far as that?

MAN: Yes, I'm afraid so. But you have a number of options to get you there and you can always rent a car right here at the airport, of course.

WOMAN: Right. Well, I don't really want to drive myself, so I'd like more information about public transport.

MAN: OK. In that case the quickest and most comfortable is a cab and of course there are always plenty available. But it'll cost you. You can also take a Greyhound bus or there's an Airport Shuttle Service to Milton. *Q1*

WOMAN: Hmmm, I think for that kind of distance a cab would be way beyond my budget. But the bus sounds OK. Can you tell me how much that would cost?

MAN: Sure. Let's see, that would be $15 one way, or $27.50 return. . . that's on the Greyhound.

WOMAN: Oh, that's quite cheap – great! But whereabouts does it stop in Milton?

MAN: It goes directly from the airport here to the City Centre and it's pretty fast. But you have to bear in mind that there is only one departure a day, so it depends what time your flight gets in. *Q2*

WOMAN: Oh, of course. Hang on, we're due to get there at 11.30 am.

MAN: Hmmm, too bad, the bus leaves at 3.45, so you would have quite a wait – more than 4 hours. *Q3*

WOMAN: Oh, I see. Well, what about the Shuttle you mentioned?

MAN: OK. That's the Airport Shuttle that will take you from the airport right to your hotel or private address. It's a door-to-door service and it would suit you much better, because there's one every two hours. *Q4*

WOMAN: So how much does that cost?

MAN: Let's see. Yeah, that's $35 one way, $65 return, so I guess it's a bit more expensive than the Greyhound.

Tapescripts

WOMAN:	Oh, that doesn't sound too bad, especially if it'll take me straight to the hotel.
MAN:	But you do need to <u>reserve a seat</u>. *Q5*
WOMAN:	OK, is it possible to make a booking right now? Through you?
MAN:	Sure.

MAN:	OK, I just have to fill this form out for you. So what date do you want to book this for?
WOMAN:	The 16th of October – oh, no, sorry, that's my departure date. <u>I arrive on the 17th</u>, so book it for then, please. *Q6*
MAN:	So, that's the Toronto Airport Shuttle to Milton. And this is for just one person or . . . ?
WOMAN:	Yes, just me, please.
MAN:	Right. And you said your expected time of arrival was 11.30? So if I book your Shuttle for after 12.00 – let's say, <u>12.30</u>: that should give you plenty of time to, you know, collect your baggage, maybe grab a coffee? *Q7*
WOMAN:	<u>Yeah, that sounds fine</u>, as long as we land on time!
MAN:	Well, we'll take your flight details so you don't need to worry too much about that. Now, what about the fare? What sort of ticket do you want? One way or . . .?
WOMAN:	Yes, that'll be fine, provided I can book the return trip once I'm there.
MAN:	No problem – just allow a couple of days in advance to make sure you get a seat. And what's your name, please?
WOMAN:	Janet, Janet Thomson.
MAN:	Is that Thompson spelt with a 'p'?
WOMAN:	No, it's <u>T-H-O-M-S-O-N</u>. *Q8*
MAN:	OK. And you'll be coming from the UK? What flight will you be travelling on?
WOMAN:	Oh, it's Air Canada flight number <u>AC936</u>, from London Heathrow. *Q9*
WMAN:	Right. Now, do you know where you'll be staying? We need to give the driver an address.
WOMAN:	Yes, it's called the Vacation Motel – and I think it's near the town centre. Anyway, the address is 24, Kitchener Street – that's KITCHENER Street.
MAN:	That's fine. Right, so that's $35 to pay please. Have you got your credit card number there?
WOMAN:	Yes, it's a VISA card, and the number is <u>3303 8450 2045 6837</u>. *Q10*
MAN:	OK. Well, that seems to be everything. Have a good trip and we'll see you in Toronto next week!
WOMAN:	Yes, bye – oh, thanks for your help!

SECTION 2

Thank you all for coming to my talk this evening. It's nice to see so many people in the audience. For those of you who don't know very much about PS Camping, let me start by giving you some background information about the company.

The company started twenty-five years ago. It actually opened as a retail chain selling camping equipment, and <u>then twenty years ago, it bought a small number of campsites in</u>   *Q11* <u>the UK, and began offering camping holidays.</u> The company grew rapidly and has been providing holidays in continental Europe for the last fifteen years.

If you book a camping holiday with us, you'll have a choice of over three hundred sites. In Italy we now have some 64 sites that we either own, or have exclusive use of. <u>France is where</u> *Q12* <u>we have the majority of sites</u>, and we currently have a project to expand into Switzerland. We also have a number of sites in Northern Spain, particularly in the mountainous region of Picos de Europa. We've upgraded all these Spanish sites, and improved them considerably from their original three-star rating.

We believe our holidays offer superb facilities for the whole family. Parents who want their children to be fully occupied for all or part of the day can take advantage of our children's activities. These are organised by our well-qualified and enthusiastic staff. Each day kicks off with a sports match, perhaps football, or volleyball, <u>followed by an hour of drama</u> for   *Q13* everyone. This may include singing or dancing, mime or other activities. In the afternoon, there's a different art activity for each day of the week including a poster competition or model making. What's more, our sites are truly child-friendly, and, with this in mind, we operate a no-noise rule in the evenings. Children's evening activities usually finish at 9.30, or occasionally 10, and <u>from 10.30 holiday-makers are expected to be quiet</u> in the areas where *Q14* there are tents.

We want nothing to go wrong on a PS Camping holiday, but if it does, we also want all customers to be insured. If you haven't organised an annual insurance policy of your own you'll need to take out the low-cost cover we offer and <u>we require that you arrange this</u>   *Q15* <u>when you make your holiday reservation.</u>

There are many advantages to choosing PS Camping, and to recommending it to others. As a regular customer, you'll be kept informed of special offers, and your friends can benefit from ten per cent off their holiday, or book a luxury tent for the price of a standard one. In return, we'll send you <u>a thank-you present</u>, which you can choose from a list of high-quality items. *Q16*

When it comes to our tents, these are equipped to the highest standard. We really do think of every essential detail, from an oven and cooking rings fuelled by bottled gas, to mirrors in the bedroom areas. If you don't want to cook indoors, <u>you can borrow a barbecue if you ask in</u> *Q17* advance for one to be made available, and there's even a picnic blanket to sit on outside your

tent. Inside, a box of games and toys can be found, and children's tents can be hired if   *Q18*
required. All tents have a fridge, and if you want to spend the day on the beach, for example,
ask for a specially designed PS Camping cool box, which will keep your food and drinks   *Q19*
chilled. There are excellent washing facilities at all our sites, with washing machines and
clothes lines in the central areas, along with mops and buckets in case your tent needs   *Q20*
cleaning during your stay. All sites have a café and/or a shop for those who'd rather 'eat in'
than dine at a local restaurant.

SECTION 3

TUTOR:	Well, you've both been looking at different styles of managing individuals in companies and the workplace. How's the research going, Philip?
PHILIP:	Well, I've been looking at why individualism, I mean individual differences, are such an important area of management studies. When you think about any organization, be it a family business or a multinational company, they are all fundamentally a group of people working together. But it's what these individuals contribute to their places of work that makes you realize how important they are. Of course they bring different ideas, but it's also their attitudes and their experiences of learning. Diversity is important in these areas too.

Q21 (aligned with "but it's also their attitudes")

TUTOR:	So why do people behave so differently from one another at work?
PHILIP:	There are lots of reasons but research has shown a lot of it comes down to personality. And the other factor is gender. It's a well known fact that men and women do lots of things in different ways, and the workplace is no different.

Q22 (aligned with "gender. It's a well known")

TUTOR:	Did you look at the effects of this variation on companies?
PHILIP:	Yes, I did. On the positive side, exposure to such diversity helps encourage creativity which is generally an asset to a company. But unfortunately individual differences are also the root of conflict between staff and they can lead to difficulties for management, which can sometimes be serious.

Q23 (aligned with "unfortunately individual differences")

TUTOR:	Thanks, Philip. So now I guess the two main things to remember here are to identify individual talent and then to utilize it. So Janice, *you* were looking at identifying different talents in workers. Do you think this is easy for managers to do?
JANICE:	Well, currently teamwork is in fashion in the workplace and in my opinion the importance of the individual is generally neglected. What managers should be targeting is those employees who can take the lead in a situation and are not afraid to accept the idea of responsibility.

Q24 (aligned with "managers should be targeting")

TUTOR:	That's true Janice but unfortunately many managers think the entire notion of encouraging individuality amongst their staff is far too hard.

JANICE:	Yes, that may be true but I think one of the most important tasks of managers is to consider the needs of the individual on one hand and group co-operation and conformity on the other. It requires creative thinking on the part of management to avoid tension.	*Q25*
TUTOR:	So Janice, what kind of people do you think companies should be looking for?	
JANICE:	Well, it has to start from the very beginning when companies are looking for new employees. When the personnel department is choosing between applicants they need to look for someone who's broken the mould and can think for themselves. Instead, people making these decisions often use a range of psychological tests to see if a person is a problem solver, or will do as they're told. I'm not convinced these qualities are actually the most important.	*Q26*
TUTOR:	So do you think being a good team player is overrated?	
JANICE:	No, it's not overrated. You do need to learn the rules and learn them fast. No individual can get around this if you're working in an organization.	
TUTOR:	So how should managers deal with this?	
JANICE:	Rewards. When an individual demonstrates the behaviour the organisation expects, some kind of incentive can be given. What's important here is that this happens right at the beginning so new recruits learn the rules of the system immediately. Also the incentive should be something the individual actually wants, and this isn't always just money.	*Q27*
TUTOR:	To come back to you, Philip. You were saying that recognition of good performers is essential. What else should managers be looking for?	
PHILIP:	Well, managing people means you not only have an understanding of your employees, but you also recognise the culture of the organization. In fact, for some organizations creativity and individuality may be the last thing they want to see during working hours!	*Q28*
TUTOR:	Very true.	
PHILIP:	Yes, but managing people isn't as easy as it looks. For example, change in the workplace can be quite tricky, especially if there's a need to increase profit. And at times like these managers may have to give priority to profit rather than individual staff needs.	*Q29*
TUTOR:	Yes, and that creates difficult situations for people.	
PHILIP:	Yes but what's important is that managers are able to deal with quite high levels of personal stress. During times of change they should be thinking not only about the strain on their staff but take time out to think of themselves.	*Q30*
TUTOR:	Absolutely. So what are the implications of that for. . .	

SECTION 4

Good afternoon, everyone!

This is the first seminar in preparation for our archaeological fieldwork in Namibia; we are fantastically lucky to have received partial research funding for this trip from our Institute, so I shall expect 200% attention and participation from you all. First in this seminar, I'm going to give a brief introduction to contemporary research on rock art, and in the second part I'm going to give you some do's and don'ts for our fieldwork trip in April – so please   *Q31* listen very carefully.

I'm first going to focus on the interpretation of rock art in Namibia. We are very fortunate to be going to an area where you can find some of the most important sites in the entire world. And I hope to show you how easy it is for everyone to make mistakes in looking at cultures which are different from our own – the first and most important lesson we have to learn.

In Namibia there are both paintings and engravings – that's where the surface of the rock is cut out. Many of the engravings show footprints of animals and most scholars used to think that the purpose of these was simple and obvious: this rock art was like a school book with pictures to teach children about tracks: which track belonged to which animal – giraffe, lion   *Q32* and so on.

But there were some mysteries. First, when you look at a typical Namibian painting or engraving, you see the tracks are repeated, there are dozens of tracks for the same animal.   *Q33* You'd expect just one clear illustration if the reason – the aim – was to teach tracking.

Now there were two more problems. Why are some of the engravings of animals *very* accurate as you'd expect – all clearly identifiable – and others quite unrealistic?

And another mystery – some of these *unrealistic* animals – that's in the engravings – seem to be half human. Some, for example, have got human faces. Many researchers now think   *Q34* that these were pictures the wise men engraved of themselves. They believed they could use   *Q35* magic to control the animals they had drawn, so the hunters could then catch them for food.

This shows you some of the dangers of coming from one culture to another, as we'll be doing, without understanding it fully. Scholars imagined that children looked at rock art pictures to learn to track – just because they themselves had learnt skills from pictures; many researchers now believe that rock art had a much more complex purpose. And we'll talk more about it next week!

Now before I invite you to join in a discussion in this second part of the seminar, I'd like to make some very important points about our fieldwork – and in fact any field trip to look at rock art.

We're going to a number of sites, and we won't always be together. The single largest problem faced by people who manage the sites is – yes, I'm sure you've guessed – damage caused by visitors, even though it's usually unintentional.

Whenever you do go to a site, don't forget you can learn many things from <u>observing at a</u>   *Q36*
<u>distance</u> instead of walking all over it. This can really help to reduce visitor pressure. People often say, 'Well, there's only two of us and just this one time', but maybe thousands of people are saying the same thing.

And then some basic rules to guide you – we'll have our own camp near a village, but remember never to camp on a site if you go on your own. It may be disrespectful to the <u>people of that culture,</u> and certainly don't make fires, however romantic it may seem. It's   *Q37*
really dangerous in dry areas, and you <u>can easily burn priceless undiscovered material</u> by   *Q38*
doing so.

So, how are we going to enjoy the rock art on our field trip? By looking at it, drawing it and photographing it – <u>NEVER by touching</u> it or even tracing it. Rock art is fragile and precious. *Q39*

Remember that climbing on rocks and in caves can destroy in a moment what has lasted for centuries. So no heroics in Namibia, please! Try to be extra careful and help others to be too.

And lastly please don't even move rocks or branches to take photographs – <u>you should leave</u>   *Q40*
<u>the site intact</u> – I'm sure I can rely on you to do that.

Well, that's about all I want to say before today's first discussion, but if you have any questions please ask them now – and don't forget you'll find some fascinating information about world-wide sites on the Internet. Right, first question then?

TEST 2

SECTION 1

WOMAN:	Hello . . . motor insurance department . . .	
MAN:	Oh hello . . . I'd like to ask about insurance for my car.	
WOMAN:	Yes, of course. I'll just take a few details. What's your name?	
MAN:	<u>Patrick Jones.</u>	*Example*
WOMAN:	And your address?	
MAN:	It's <u>27 Bank Road.</u>	*Q1*
WOMAN:	27 Bank Road. Is that in Greendale?	
MAN:	Yes.	
WOMAN:	And what's your daytime phone number?	
MAN:	My work number is 730453.	
WOMAN:	And could I ask what your occupation is?	
MAN:	<u>Dentist.</u>	*Q2*

WOMAN:	OK . . . now a few details about your car . . . What size is the engine?	
MAN:	It's 1200 ccs.	
WOMAN:	Thank you . . . and the make and model?	
MAN:	It's a Hewton Sable.	
WOMAN:	Could you spell the model name please?	
MAN:	Yes . . . S-A-B-L-E.	*Q3*
WOMAN:	Ah yes . . . thanks. And when was it made?	
MAN:	1997.	
WOMAN:	Lovely . . . right . . . I presume you've had a previous insurer?	
MAN:	Yes.	
WOMAN:	Right . . . we need to know the name of the company.	
MAN:	Yes . . . it was Northern Star.	*Q4*
WOMAN:	Thank you, and have you made any insurance claims in the last five years?	
MAN:	Yes . . . one in 1999.	
WOMAN:	And what was the problem?	
MAN:	It was stolen . . . but . . .	*Q5*
WOMAN:	That's fine, Mr Jones . . . that's all we need to know at the moment . . .	

WOMAN:	And will there be any other named drivers?	
MAN:	Just the one . . .	
WOMAN:	And his name?	
MAN:	Simon Paynter.	
WOMAN:	Could you spell the surname please?	
MAN:	P-A-Y-N-T-E-R.	*Q6*
WOMAN:	OK thank you . . . And what relationship is he to you?	
MAN:	He's my brother-in-law.	*Q7*
WOMAN:	And what will you or Mr Paynter be using the car for?	
MAN:	Well . . . mainly for social use . . .	
WOMAN:	Social use *(murmuring)*. Will you be using it to travel to work?	*Q8*
MAN:	Yes . . . sometimes.	
WOMAN:	. . . Anything else?	
MAN:	No. That's it . . .	
WOMAN:	And finally . . . when would you like to start the insurance?	
MAN:	I'll need it from the 31st of January.	
WOMAN:	Right . . . Mr Jones . . . I'm getting a couple of quotes coming up on the computer now . . . and the best bet looks like being with a company called Red Flag.	*Q9*
MAN:	Yeah.	
WOMAN:	And that comes out at $450 per year . . .	*Q10*
MAN:	Well . . . that seems OK . . . it's quite a bit lower than I've been paying up to now . . .	
WOMAN:	Great . . . so would you like me to go ahead with that?	
MAN:	Sure . . . why not?	
WOMAN:	How would you like to pay?	

SECTION 2

Thank you for calling the Tourist Line. There are many different ways of getting round the city and we'd like to suggest some you may not have thought of.

How about a city trip by boat? There are four main stopping points – from west to east: stop A Green Banks, stop B City Bridge, stop C Roman Landing and stop D Newtown.   *Q11 Q12*

You can find the main booking office at stop A.

The first boat leaves at 8 a.m. and the last one at 6.30 p.m. There are also many attractions   *Q13*
you can visit along the river. At Stop A, if you have time, you can visit the fine 16th century palace here built for the king with its beautiful formal gardens. It's very near the booking   *Q14*
office. Now *you* can enjoy every corner of this superb residence.

Stop B Why don't you visit Tower Restaurant with its wide range of refreshments? This is a   *Q15*
place where you can sit and enjoy the wonderful views over the old commercial and banking   *Q16*
centre of the city.

Stop C is the area where, in the first century AD, invading soldiers crossed the river; this was much shallower than it is now. That's why this area is called Roman Landing. There's an interactive Museum to visit here with a large shop which has a good range of local history   *Q17*
books.

At the furthest point of the trip, stop D, the most exciting place to visit is the new Entertainment Complex with seven-screen cinema, bowling alley and video games arcade.   *Q18*

Besides the boat tours, there are city buses. Two companies offer special services:

The Top Bus Company runs all its tours with a live commentary in English. Tours leave from 8.30 a.m. every 20 minutes. There are departures from Central Station, Castle Hill   *Q19*
and Long Walk. This is a hop-on hop-off service and tickets are valid for 24 hours.
For further details call Top Bus on 0208 9447810.

The Number One Sightseeing Tour is available with a commentary in eight languages. Buses depart from Central Station every five to six minutes from about 9 a.m. with the last bus at   *Q20*
around 7 p.m. There are also Number One services with an English-speaking . . .

SECTION 3

INTERVIEWER: We're pleased to welcome Dr Martin Merrywhether of the Antarctic
                  Centre in Christchurch, New Zealand who has come along to talk to
                  us today about the role of the Centre and the Antarctic Treaty.
INTERVIEWER: Now my first question is about the choice of location for the centre.
                  Why Christchurch? Was it because of the climate?

DOCTOR:	Well actually New Zealand is the second closest country to Antarctica and Christchurch is often used on Antarctic expeditions.	*Q21*
INTERVIEWER:	Right, so it's because of where we are . . . coupled with our historical role. So tell us – what is the main purpose of the centre?	
DOCTOR:	Well . . . we have two complementary roles. One is as a scientific base for expeditions and research and the other is as an information centre.	
INTERVIEWER:	Tell us something about the role as a scientific base.	
DOCTOR:	We're able to provide information about what scientists should take with them to the South Pole – for example, the centre contains a clothing warehouse where expeditions are supplied with suitable clothing for the extreme conditions.	*Q22*
INTERVIEWER:	I suppose you need a bit more than your normal winter coat!	
DOCTOR:	Yes, exactly and then there's also the specialist library and mapping services.	
INTERVIEWER:	Right. And which countries are actually located at the centre?	
DOCTOR:	Well . . . the centre houses research programmes for New Zealand, for The United States as well as for Italy . . . there's even a US post office at the American airforce base here.	
INTERVIEWER:	Really? And what does the visitor's centre offer?	
DOCTOR:	Well, since very few people will ever experience the Antarctic first hand, the visitors' centre aims to recreate the atmosphere of Antarctica. There's a mock camp site where you can see inside an Antarctic tent and imagine yourself sleeping there. And the centre also acts as a showcase for the unique international co-operation which exists in Antarctica today.	*Q23*
INTERVIEWER:	What is it actually like at the South Pole? I know you've been there on a number of occasions.	
DOCTOR:	Yes, I have and each time I'm struck by the awesome beauty of the place. It's magnificent but you can really only visit it in the summer months.	*Q24*
INTERVIEWER:	October to March.	
DOCTOR:	Yes, because it's completely dark for four months of the year (*pause*) . . . and in addition it has to be the coldest place on earth.	
INTERVIEWER:	Colder than the North Pole? Why's that?	
DOCTOR:	Well, unlike the North Pole, which is actually a frozen sea, Antarctica is a land mass shaped like a dome, with the result that the winds blow down the slopes at speeds of up to 150 km an hour and that's what makes it so cold. And one other interesting thing is that Antarctica is the driest continent on earth, surprisingly, and so you have to drink large amounts of water when you're there.	*Q25*
INTERVIEWER:	How old is Antarctica?	
DOCTOR:	We're pretty sure it was part of a larger land mass but it broke away from the rest of the continent 170 million years ago.	
INTERVIEWER:	How can you be certain of this?	

DOCTOR:	. . . because fossils and rocks have been discovered in Antarctica which are the same as those found in places such as Africa and Australia.	*Q26*
INTERVIEWER:	Amazing . . . To think that it was once attached to Africa . . .	

- -

INTERVIEWER:	Now let's just have a look at the Antarctic Treaty. How far back does the idea of an international treaty go?	
DOCTOR:	Well, as far back as the 19th century, when eleven nations organised an international event.	
INTERVIEWER:	When was that exactly?	
DOCTOR:	In 1870. And it was called the Polar Research Meeting. And then, not long after that, they organised something called the First International Polar Year.	
INTERVIEWER:	And that took place when exactly?	
DOCTOR:	Over two years from 1882 to 1883. But it wasn't until the 1950s that the idea of an international treaty was proposed. And in 1959 the Treaty was actually signed.	*Q27* *Q28*
INTERVIEWER:	What do you see as the main achievements of the treaty?	
DOCTOR:	Well, firstly it means that the continent is reserved for peaceful use.	*Q29 Q30*
INTERVIEWER:	That's Article 1, isn't it?	
DOCTOR:	Yes . . .	
INTERVIEWER:	That's important since the territory belongs to everyone.	
DOCTOR:	Yes but not as important as Article 5, which prohibits any nuclear explosions or waste disposal.	*Q29 Q30*
INTERVIEWER:	Which is marvellous. Well, I'm afraid we're going to have to stop there because I'm afraid we've run out of time. Thanks for coming along today and telling us all about the centre and its work.	

SECTION 4

My topic is handedness – whether in different sports it is better to be left- or right-sided or whether a more balanced approach is more successful. I'm left-handed myself and I actually didn't see any relevance to my own life when I happened to start reading an article by a sports psychologist called Peter Matthews. He spent the first part of the article talking about handedness in music instead of sport, which I have to say almost put me off from reading further. But what I soon became struck by was the sheer volume of both observation and *Q31* investigation he had done in many different sports and I felt persuaded that what he had to say would be of real interest. I think Matthews' findings will be beneficial, not so much in helping sportspeople to work on their weaker side, but more that they can help them *Q32* identify the most suitable strategies to use in a given game. Although most trainers know how important handedness is, at present they are rather reluctant to make use of the *Q33* insights scientists like Matthews can give, which I think is rather short-sighted because focusing on individual flexibility is only part of the story.

Anyway, back to the article.

Matthews found a German study which looked at what he called 'mixed-handedness', that is, the capacity to use both left and right hands equally. It looked at mixed-handedness in 40 musicians on a variety of instruments. Researchers examined a number of variables, e.g. type of instrument played, regularity of practice undertaken and length of time playing instrument . . . and found the following: keyboard players had high levels of mixed-handedness, whereas string players like cellists and violinists strongly favoured one hand. Also those who started younger were more mixed-handed.   *Q34*

Matthews also reports studies of handedness in apes. Apes get a large proportion of their food by 'fishing' ants from ant hills. The studies show that apes, like humans, show handedness – though for them right- and left-handedness is about equal, whereas about 85% of humans are right-handed. Studies showed that apes consistently using the same hand   *Q35* fished out 30% more ants than those varying between the two.

Matthews started researching several different sports and found different types of handedness in each. By the way, he uses 'handedness' to refer to the dominant side for feet and eyes as well as hands. Anyway, his team measured the hand, feet and eyes of 2,611 players and found that there were really three main types of laterality: mixed – you work equally well on both sides – both hand and eye; single – you tend to favour one side but both hand and eye favour the same side; and cross-laterality – a player's hands and eyes favour only one side but they are opposite sides. Let's start with hockey. Matthews found that it was best to be mixed-handed – this is because a hockey stick must be deployed in two directions – it would be a   *Q36* drawback to have hand or eye favouring one side. An interesting finding is that mixed-handed hockey players were significantly more confident than their single-handed counterparts.   *Q37* Things are slightly different in racket sports like tennis. Here the important thing is to have the dominant hand and eye on the one side. This means that there is a bigger area of vision   *Q38* on the side where most of the action occurs. If a player is cross lateral the racket is invisible from the dominant eye for much of the swing. It means that they can only make corrections   *Q39* much later . . . and often the damage has been done by then.

And moving to a rather different type of sport which involves large but precise movements – gymnastics. It's been found that cross hand-eye favouring is best. The predominant reason for this is because it aids balance – which is of course absolutely central to performance in this   *Q40* sport.

TEST 3

SECTION 1

AGENT:	Good morning.
STUDENT:	Oh, good morning. Is this . . . er . . . room number 26?
AGENT:	Yes, that's right.
STUDENT:	So is this the Student Job Centre?
AGENT:	It certainly is. How can I help you?
STUDENT:	Well, actually I'm looking for a job – a part-time job. Do you have anything available at the moment?
AGENT:	Ah, yes . . . Are you a registered student? I'm afraid this service is only available to full-time students.
STUDENT:	Yes . . . I am. I'm doing a degree in Business Studies. Here's my student card.
AGENT:	Which year are you in?
STUDENT:	Well . . . I've been at uni for four years but I'm in the Third Year because I took last year off.
AGENT:	Right . . . well, let's just have a look at what positions are available at the moment. There's a job working at the reception desk at the Sports Centre, for three evenings a week – that's Wednesdays, Thursdays and Fridays.
STUDENT:	That sounds like fun but unfortunately I have evening lectures – so that's not possible, I'm afraid. Is there anything during the day?
AGENT:	OK, that's no good then. Um. What about cleaning? There's a position for a cleaner at the Child Care Centre.
STUDENT:	Right . . .
AGENT:	But you'd need to be there at 6 am. Does that appeal?
STUDENT:	Six o'clock in the morning! Oh, that's far too early for me, I'm afraid. I'd never make it that early in the morning.
AGENT:	Mmm . . . Well – there was a position going in the Computer Lab. for three days a week that might be OK. Ah, here it is! No, it's in the Library, not the Lab., Clerical Assistant required – I think it mostly involves putting the books back on the shelves. Oh no – hang on. It's for Wednesday and Friday evenings again.
STUDENT:	No – I can't manage that because of the lectures.
AGENT:	OK, I'm getting the idea. Look, I'll just get a few details from you anyway, and then we can check through the list and see what comes up.

The right-hand margin labels: *Example* (aligned with "a part-time job"), *Q1*, *Q2*, *Q3*, *Q4*, *Q5*.

AGENT:	We'll fill in the personal details on this application form first, if that's OK?
STUDENT:	Yes, that's fine.
AGENT:	Now, what's your name again?

STUDENT:	Anita Newman – that's N-E-W-M-A-N.	
AGENT:	And your address, Anita?	
STUDENT:	I'm in one of the Halls of Residence for post-graduate students, you know, <u>International House.</u>	*Q6*
AGENT:	OK – that's easy. What's your room number there?	
STUDENT:	Room B569 – no sorry <u>B659.</u> I always get that wrong. I haven't been living there very long.	*Q7*
AGENT:	Do you have any other skills? Typing, languages, that sort of thing?	
STUDENT:	Well, I speak some Japanese.	
AGENT:	Right, I'll make a note of that. Now – let's see what else is available. What do you think of administrative work? There is a position for an <u>Office Assistant</u> at the English Language Centre.	*Q8*
STUDENT:	That sounds interesting.	
AGENT:	It's for 3 days a week – Monday, Friday and Saturday mornings. Interested?	
STUDENT:	Mmm. I was hoping to have Saturdays free. But I need the work so . . . can you tell me what the job involves?	
AGENT:	Yes, sure. It says here that you'll be required to deal with student enquiries and <u>answer the phone.</u>	*Q9*
STUDENT:	I'm sure I can handle all that without a problem.	
AGENT:	Great. Well, would you like me to arrange an interview for you? Say, Friday morning, around ten?	
STUDENT:	Could we make it a bit later? Unfortunately, I've got something to do at ten. Would that be OK?	
AGENT:	Not a problem. <u>How about eleven thirty?</u> Hope it works out for you Anita.	*Q10*
STUDENT:	Me too. And thanks for all your help.	

SECTION 2

Good morning. I'm very pleased to have been invited along to your club to talk about our Charity Sponsored Walking Holiday for Education Aid. I'll start by giving you a brief overview of what it entails. First of all let me explain what we mean by 'sponsored' here. This is where people promise to donate money to the charity if you achieve your goal, in this case to walk a certain number of miles.

Basically we are organizing a ten-day holiday, from the sixth to the sixteenth of November, with <u>eight days actual walking</u>, trekking in the Semira Mountains. *Q11*

Let's have a look at some of the details. We require you to raise sponsorship money of at least $3,200, paying $250 of it up front as a deposit and the rest in stages throughout the year. Out of this about thirty-five per cent will go on your expenses, and that leaves <u>sixty-five per cent</u> guaranteed to go to the charity. *Q12*

Which brings me to the most important part. This trek is being specifically organized to help education in the Semira region. Last year we helped train teachers for the disabled, and this year we're focusing on the pupils. Each of the walkers' sponsorship money will go to help an *Q13* individual special needs pupil in one of the mountain schools. In the second part of the talk I'll be giving you a lot more details, but back to the basic information.

Age limits. This is the second time we have run this kind of holiday and um, on the first we even had an eighty-year old, but we found it was wise to establish limits this time. You have to be at least eighteen and the top limit is now seventy, though you need to obtain a health certificate from your doctor if you are over sixty years old.

Now, the Semira Mountains are among the highest in the world but you mustn't be too daunted, we will mainly be trekking in the foothills only, although there will be spectacular views even in the foothills. However, you will need to be extremely fit if you aren't now and *Q14* you're interested in coming with us. You have plenty of time to get into shape. You will be sleeping in tents so you must have quite a bit of equipment with you but you will be helped by local assistants. Your bedding and so forth will be carried by them. We ask that you only *Q15* walk with a small rucksack with needs for the day.

I don't think I've really said enough about the marvellous area you'll be walking in. Let's have a look at some of the sights you'll be seeing. Apart from these spectacular snow-covered peaks and valleys, there are marvellous historic villages. The area has been famous for centuries for making beautiful carpets, although recently there has been a trend to move *Q16* into weaving blankets and wood carving. The people are extremely friendly and welcoming. We deliberately keep the parties small in size to minimize disruption to people and landscape.

I hope that there are still some people interested. I will be distributing leaflets at the end where you can find out more information, but just for the moment I'll outline the itinerary, the main high points of the holiday. Obviously, you'll start by flying out to Kishba, the capital city, on Day One. After a couple of days to acclimatize yourself, you'll start the trek on Day Three walking through the enormous Katiba Forest which will take the whole of the *Q17* day. Day Four takes us higher up, going through the foothills past a number of villages and visiting a school for the disabled in Sohan. Then you have a rest day, that's Day Five, before going to the spectacular Kumi Temple with twelfth-century carvings, set in a small forest by *Q18* a lake and that's Day Six, the highlight for many. We stay near there for Day Seven because then comes the hardest day, walking through very mountainous country, but culminating in a swim in the Parteh Falls. This is the highest waterfall in the region. Day Nine is much easier, *Q19* with part of the day spent in a village where they make some of the gorgeous red blankets. *Q20* Then back down to Kishba and the journey home.

So you can see it's a pretty packed timetable . . .

SECTION 3

SIMON:	Thanks to all of you for coming along today to hear about how the robotic float project is helping with ocean research. Well, first of all we'll look at what a robotic float does and its use. So let's start with the device itself. It looks a bit like a cigar and it's about one and a half *Q21* metres long. More importantly it's full of equipment that's designed to collect data. So, it can help us in building up a profile of different factors which work together within the world's oceans.
STUDENT 1:	Sounds like a big project – isn't it too big for one country to undertake?
SIMON:	That's quite true but this project is a really good example of international co-operation. Over the last five years scientists from thirteen countries have been taking part in the project and launching *Q22* floats in their area of ocean control. And next year this number will rise to fourteen when Indonesia joins the project.
STUDENT 2:	That's impressive.
SIMON:	But let's move onto how floats work.
SIMON:	The operational cycle goes like this. Each of the floats is dropped in the ocean from a boat at a set point and activated from a satellite. *Q23* Then the float immediately sinks about 2,000 metres. . . that's two whole kilometres down in the water. It stays at this depth for about 10 days and is carried around by the currents which operate in the ocean at this level. During this time it's possible for it to cover quite large distances but the average is fifty kilometres. *Q24*
STUDENT 2:	So what is it actually recording?
SIMON:	Well at this stage nothing, but as it rises to the surface it collects all sorts of data, most importantly variations in salinity, that's salt levels, and the changes in temperature, a bit like underwater weather balloons. *Q25* Then when it gets back to the surface all the data it's collected is beamed up to the satellite. After about five hours on the surface the float automatically sinks, beginning the whole process again.
STUDENT 1:	What happens to the data?
SIMON:	Well the information is transferred direct to onshore meteorological stations. . . like our one in Hobart. . . and within four hours the findings can be on computers and they can be mapped and analysed.

STUDENT 2:	You say you're building models of the world's ocean systems but how're they going to be used, and more importantly, when?
SIMON:	Some of the data has already helped in completing projects. For *Q26* example, our understanding of the underlying causes of El Niño events is being confirmed by float data. Another way we're using float data is to help us to understand the mechanics of climate change, like *Q27* global warming and ozone depletion. That's part of an ongoing variability study but the results are still a long way off.

| | However, this is not the case with our ocean weather forecasting. Because we know from the floats what the prevailing weather conditions will be in certain parts of the ocean, we can advise the navy on search and rescue missions. That's happening right now and many yachtsmen owe their lives to the success of this project. In addition, the float data can help us to look at the biological implications of ocean processes. | *Q28* |

STUDENT 1: Would that help with preserving fish stocks? *Q29*

SIMON: Yes, and advising governments on fisheries legislation. We're well on the way to completing a project on this. We hope it will help to bring about more sustainable fishing practices. We'll be seeing the results of that quite soon.

STUDENT 2: It sounds like the data from floats has lots of applications.

SIMON: Yes it does. It's also a powerful agricultural tool. If we were aware of what the weather would be like, say, next year, we could make sure that the farmers planted appropriate grain varieties to produce the best yield from the available rainfall.

STUDENT 1: That sounds a bit like science fiction, especially when now we can't even tell them when a drought will break.

SIMON: I agree that this concept is still a long way in the future, but it will *Q30* come eventually and the float data will have made a contribution.

SECTION 4

Good morning everyone. Today's lecture forms part of the Hospitality and Tourism module. Last week I looked at the economy end of the hotel business; this week I'm going to discuss the luxury end of the market. Let's consider the following scenario . . .

You wake up in the middle of the night in a strange hotel miles away from home, disoriented most probably from jet lag, when even the most expensive surroundings can seem empty and *Q31* dispiriting. You have paid a great deal of money to stay in this first-class hotel with its contemporary technology, but according to recent research carried out by an international travel and public relations company, all is not well. The research suggests that even the most opulent, luxurious hotels seem to have underestimated the most basic needs of their customers – be they travelling for work or pleasure: the need to feel at home in surroundings *Q32* which are both familiar and inviting.

Do these findings, however, apply only to hotels situated in particular areas? Is it possible that the external environment can affect a guest's well-being? The company's research covered a whole range of different hotel types, both independent hotels and those which are part of *Q33* large chains. They investigated chic so-called boutique hotels in the heart of downtown business districts, stately mansions located in the depths of beautiful countryside, and plush hotels built at the edge of tropical beaches surrounded by palm trees and idyllic blue ocean. And the research concluded that what was *outside* the hotel building simply didn't matter. *Q34* This is a fascinating revelation and those of you hoping to move into careers in the travel and leisure industry would be well advised to look at the findings in more detail.

But back to the main point of this lecture . . . the need to feel at home. What can the hotel industry do about it? And is the very idea so subjective that it's impossible to do *anything* about it on a global basis?

However, nothing stands still in this world. One company has come up with the slogan 'Take Your Home With You', and aims to provide clients with luxury serviced apartments. Those in the business travel industry maintain that these serviced apartments dispense with all the unwanted and expensive hotel services that business travellers don't want, while maximising   *Q35* the facilities they do want. For example, not only sleeping and living accommodation, but also a sleek modern kitchen that allows guests to cook and entertain if they wish, at no   *Q36* additional cost. The attractions of such facilities are obvious and it'll be interesting to see whether the company manages to establish a trend all over the world and make a lasting   *Q37* impact on the luxury accommodation market.

Now, finally I want to consider the psychology underpinning the traditional holiday hotel industry. As a hotelier, how do you go about attracting people to give up the security of their own home and entrust themselves to staying in a completely strange place and sleeping in an unfamiliar bed? Firstly, hotels exploit people's need to escape the predictability of their   *Q38* everyday lives. For a few days people can pretend they are free of responsibilities and can indulge themselves. Secondly, there is something very powerful in our need to be pampered and looked after, it's almost as if we return to being a baby, when everything was done for us *Q39* and we felt safe and secure. And not far removed from this is the pleasure in being spoilt and given little treats – like the miniscule bottles of shampoo and tiny bars of soap, the   *Q40* chocolate on your pillow at night – and we actually forget that we are paying for it all!

Next week, I'm going to look at eco-hotels, a fairly new phenomenon but increasingly popular . . .

TEST 4

SECTION 1

OFFICER:	Yes, what can I do for you?
STUDENT:	My friend is in homestay . . . and she really enjoys it . . . so I'd like to join a family as well.
OFFICER:	Okay, so let me get some details. What's your name?
STUDENT:	My name is Keiko Yuichini.
OFFICER:	Could you spell your family name for me?
STUDENT:	It's . . . Yuichini, that's Y-U-I-C-H-I-N-I. *Example*
OFFICER:	And your first name?
STUDENT:	It's Keiko. K-E-I-K-O. *Q1*

OFFICER:	That's Keiko Yuichini . . . okay . . . and you're female. And your nationality?
STUDENT:	I'm Japanese.
OFFICER:	Right and could I see your passport, please?
STUDENT:	Here it is . . .
OFFICER:	Okay . . . your passport number is <u>JO 6337</u> . . . And you're how old?
STUDENT:	I'm twenty-eight years old.
OFFICER:	Now, you live at one of the colleges . . . which one?
STUDENT:	Willow College, umm . . . Room 21C
OFFICER:	Right, 21C Willow College, and how long are you planning on staying with homestay?
STUDENT:	<u>About four months</u> . . . longer if I like it . . .
OFFICER:	And what course are you enrolled in?
STUDENT:	Well, I've enrolled for twenty weeks in the . . . um . . . <u>Advanced English Studies</u> because I need help with my writing . . . and I'm nearly at the end of my first five-week course.

Q2 appears beside the passport number line; Q3 beside the four months line; Q4 beside the Advanced English Studies line.

OFFICER:	Okay . . . Do you have any preference for a family with children or without children?
STUDENT:	I prefer . . . I mean I like young children, but <u>I'd like to be with older people</u> . . . you know . . . adults . . . someone around my age.
OFFICER:	Okay, and <u>what about pets</u>?
STUDENT:	<u>I am a veterinarian so that's fine</u> . . . the more the better.
OFFICER:	All right, now what about you? Are you a vegetarian or do you have any special food requirements?
STUDENT:	No, I am not a vegetarian . . . but I don't eat a lot of meat . . . <u>I really like seafood.</u>
OFFICER:	And what are your hobbies?
STUDENT:	I like reading and going to the movies.
OFFICER:	Do you play any sports?
STUDENT:	Yes, I joined the handball team, but I didn't like that . . . so I stopped playing. <u>Now I play tennis</u> on the weekend with my friends . . .
OFFICER:	All right, let's see, name, age, now the location. Are you familiar with the public transport system?
STUDENT:	No . . . I'm not really because I have been living on campus . . . I've been to the city a few times on the bus, but they are always late.
OFFICER:	What about the trains?
STUDENT:	<u>I like catching the train</u> . . . they are much faster . . .
OFFICER:	Now, let me go check on the computer and see who I've got . . . Listen, leave it with me . . . I'll check my records and <u>I'll give you details this afternoon.</u>
STUDENT:	Thank you for helping me . . .
OFFICER:	It's a pleasure. Bye.
STUDENT:	Bye.

Q5 appears beside the older people line; Q6 beside the pets line; Q7 beside the seafood line; Q8 beside the tennis line; Q9 beside the trains line; Q10 beside the give you details line.

SECTION 2

Welcome to all of you . . . can everybody see and hear me? . . . Good . . . I'm Sally, your guide for this tour of the Bicentennial Park . . . I hope that you're all wearing your most   *Q11* comfortable shoes and that you can keep up the pace. So let's get under way on our tour around this wonderful park.

I'll start today with some general background information. There used to be a lot of   *Q12* factories in this area until the 1960s. Creating the park required the demolition of lots of derelict buildings on the site, so most of the exciting park space all around you was originally warehouses and storehouses.

The idea of building a public park here was first discussed when a property developer proposed a high-rise housing development, but the local community wasn't happy. If the land was to be cleaned up, they wanted to use the site for recreation. Residents wanted   *Q13* open space for outdoor activities, rather than housing or even an indoor sports complex.

Now to the Bicentennial Park itself. It has two areas, a nature reserve and a formal park with man-made features and gardens. The tall blue-and-white building in front of us is called The Tower and is the centre point for the formal gardens. It stands twelve metres high, so follow   *Q14* me up the stairs to where we can take advantage of the fantastic views.

Well, here we are at the top of The Tower, and we're going to look at the view from each direction. Out to the east, the large buildings about a kilometre away are on the Olympic site. There's an indoor arena for gymnastics, a stadium for track and field and a swimming pool for races and synchronised swimming and also diving. If you look carefully down there, you can see the train lines. The Olympic site has its own station to encourage the use of public transport. There is also a car park, but it only holds a limited number of cars.   *Q15*

The formal park has some specially-created water features. If you look out here to the south, you can see a circular ornamental pond.

And around to the west, you can relax and sit on a bench to smell the flowers in the rose   *Q16* garden, and finally up to the north, if you look in front of you now, there's a lake with a small island in the centre, you can hire rowing boats at the boat shed, which you can't see from here, but if you look through the trees, you can see the café, which has lovely views across the   *Q17* water. OK, let's climb down now. We will go now and have a look at the nature reserve section of the park, which has opened up natural wetland to the public.

The Mangroves have been made more accessible to visitors by the boardwalk built during the park's upgrade. You'd think that people would come here to look at the unusual plant life of the area, but in fact it's more often used for cycling and is very popular with the local clubs.   *Q18*

This is the far end of the park and over there you can see the Frog Pond, a natural feature here long before the park was designed. Just next to it we have our outdoor classroom, a favourite spot for school parties. The area is now most often used by primary schools for biology lessons.

Q19

And finally let's pass by the Waterbird Refuge. This area is in a sheltered part of the estuary, that's why the park's viewing shelter is a favourite spot for bird watchers who can use it to spy through binoculars. You can watch a variety of water birds, but most visitors expect to see black swans when they come to the shelter. You might spot one yourself right now!

Q20

Well, here we are back at our starting point, the Visitor Centre.

SECTION 3

JULIE:	Remind me, Trevor . . . how long is the presentation?	
TREVOR:	Dr White said three per hour.	
JULIE:	So about twenty minutes?	
TREVOR:	Well . . . it'll be fifteen minutes per presentation.	
JULIE:	And five minutes for questions.	*Q21*
TREVOR:	And is this one going to be assessed?	*Q22*
JULIE:	No . . . not this time round . . . because it's the first one . . . you know.	
TREVOR:	Good news.	
JULIE:	Well, Trevor, what are we going to include?	
TREVOR:	Well . . . Do you think we ought to give some historical background?	
JULIE:	Oh no . . . definitely not . . . we won't have time!	
TREVOR:	OK . . . but I think we ought to say something about the geographical location . . . cos not a lot of people know where the islands are . . .	*Q23*
JULIE:	Yes . . . OK . . . I'll take notes, shall I?	
TREVOR:	Yeah, that'll be a help . . .	
JULIE:	So . . . geographical location . . .	
TREVOR:	Then we ought to give an overview of the whole education system.	
JULIE:	Shouldn't we say something about the economy . . . you know agricultural produce . . . minerals and so forth?	
TREVOR:	Well . . . Dr White said we shouldn't go into that sort of detail.	
JULIE:	But it's pretty important when you think about it . . . you know because it does influence the education system . . .	*Q24*
TREVOR:	Look . . . let's think about that one later shall we? Let's see how we're doing for time . . .	
JULIE:	OK . . . so . . . general overview of education	*Q25*
TREVOR:	Of course . . . and then the role of English language . . .	*Q26*
JULIE:	Nope . . . that goes in the Language Policy Seminar . . . don't you remember?	
TREVOR:	Are you sure?	
JULIE:	Positive.	

TREVOR:	All right . . . so those are the topics we're going to be . . . to be covering . . .

JULIE:	We need to think about what to prepare . . . Dr White said he wanted us to use plenty of visuals and things and we might as well try them out when we're not being assessed . . .	
TREVOR:	Well, the most important thing is the <u>overhead projector</u> . . .	*Q27*
JULIE:	No problem . . . <u>we'll get that from the media room</u> . . . must remember to book it . . .	
TREVOR:	Well . . . we'll need a map of course.	
JULIE:	Probably two . . . one of the islands . . . large scale.	
TREVOR:	And one of West Africa.	
JULIE:	Well, the West African one is no problem . . . <u>There's one in the Resources Room.</u>	*Q28*
TREVOR:	Oh yeah, of course, the resources room; the islands are going to be more of a problem.	
JULIE:	Tell you what . . . there's a very clear map of Santiago in that tourist brochure I showed you last week. Don't you remember it?	
TREVOR:	Oh yeah . . . that's right; we can just use the tourist brochure.	
JULIE:	We also need statistics . . . on several different things.	
TREVOR:	Literacy rates.	
JULIE:	Yes, and school places.	
TREVOR:	How about the encyclopaedia?	
JULIE:	Nah . . . not up-to-date enough!	
TREVOR:	Mmm . . . <u>why don't we call the embassy?</u>	*Q29*
JULIE:	Oh . . . someone's enthusiastic!	
TREVOR:	Well . . . if something's worth doing . . .	
JULIE:	I know . . . it's worth doing well . . . <u>OK.</u>	
TREVOR:	We can find out <u>statistics on school places</u> from them as well.	*Q30*
JULIE:	Might as well.	
TREVOR:	Look, Julie, it's almost time for our tutorials . . . we can meet again on Monday . . . but we need to prepare some stuff before then . . .	

SECTION 4

In today's lecture, I'm going to talk about Monosodium Glutamate, or MSG, as it's more commonly known. Now, MSG as you probably know, is a flavour enhancer which is used particularly in Chinese and Japanese cooking. Today I am going to explore why it is so popular in these cuisines and, more importantly, <u>how does it enhance the flavour of food?</u> *Q31*

The main reason why MSG is more commonly used in Japanese meals is tradition. For many thousands of years the Japanese have incorporated a type of seaweed known as *kombu* in their cooking, as they discovered it had the ability to make food taste better. But it wasn't

until 1908 that the ingredient in *kombu* which was responsible for the improvement in flavour
was <u>actually discovered to be glutamate</u> by scientists working there.   *Q32*

From 1908 until 1956, glutamate was produced commercially in Japan by a very slow and
expensive means of extraction. It was in 1956 that the speed of the process was improved,
and <u>industrial production increased dramatically</u> and still continues to increase to this day.   *Q33*
In fact, hundreds of thousands of tonnes of MSG are produced all over the world today.

So what exactly is MSG? Well, Monosodium Glutamate contains seventy-eight point two per
cent glutamate, twelve point two per cent sodium and <u>nine point six per cent water.</u>   *Q34*
Glutamate is an amino acid that can be found naturally in all protein-containing foods, erm,
so this includes food such as <u>meat and cheese.</u>   *Q35 Q36*

It is widely known that Chinese and Japanese food contains MSG but many people don't
seem to be aware that it is also used in foods in other parts of the world. For example it is
found in commercially made Italian pizzas, in American fast food and in Britain MSG is used
in things like potato crisps.

So, how exactly does MSG work? Well, in the Western world, we commonly talk of four
'tastes', and I'm sure you're all familiar with the concepts of sweet, sour, bitter and salt. Well,
in 1908, Kikunae Ikeda <u>identified a fifth 'taste'.</u> And it is thought that MSG intensifies this   *Q37*
naturally occurring 'taste' in some food. It does make perfect evolutionary sense that we
should have the ability to detect or taste glutamate because <u>it is the amino acid which is</u>   *Q38*
<u>most common in natural foods.</u>

John Prescott, an associate professor at the University of Chicago, suggests that this fifth
taste serves a purpose just as the other tastes do. He suggests that it signals to us the presence
of protein in food, in the same way that sweetness indicates that a food contains energy-giving
carbohydrates. <u>Bitterness</u>, he says, <u>alerts us of toxins in the food</u>, while sourness warns us of *Q39*
spoilage and <u>saltiness signals the presence of minerals.</u>   *Q40*

So, what else do we know about this fifth taste . . .

Listening and Reading Answer keys

TEST 1

LISTENING

Section 1, Questions 1–10

1	(a) taxi/cab
2	city centre/center
3	wait
4	door-to-door
5	reserve (a seat)
6	(the) 17th(of) October
7	12.30
8	Thomson
9	AC 936
10	3303 8450 2045 6837

Section 2, Questions 11–20

11	B
12	A
13	B
14	C
15	C
16	A
17	C
18	A
19	C
20	B

Section 3, Questions 21–30

21	attitude(s)
22	gender/sex
23	creativity/creativeness
24	A
25	B
26	A
27	B
28	culture
29	profit(s)
30	stress/strain

Section 4, Questions 31–40

31	April
32	children
33	repeated
34	human
35	magic
36	distance
37	culture
38	fire(s)
39	touching
40	intact

If you score . . .

0–11	12–27	28–40
you are unlikely to get an acceptable score under examination conditions and we recommend that you spend a lot of time improving your English before you take IELTS.	you may get an acceptable score under examination conditions but we recommend that you think about having more practice or lessons before you take IELTS.	you are likely to get an acceptable score under examination conditions but remember that different institutions will find different scores acceptable.

ACADEMIC READING

Reading Passage 1, Questions 1–13

1	B
2	A
3	A
4	E
5	D
6	phantom
7	echoes/obstacles
8	depth
9	submarines
10	natural selection
11	radio waves/echoes
12	mathematical theories
13	zoologist

Reading Passage 2, Questions 14–26

14	xi
15	vii
16	v
17	i
18	ix
19	ii
20	x
21	NO
22	YES
23	NOT GIVEN
24	NO
25	YES
26	NOT GIVEN

Reading Passage 3, Questions 27–40

27	D
28	A
29	B
30	C
31	FALSE
32	FALSE
33	TRUE
34	NOT GIVEN
35	NOT GIVEN
36	TRUE
37	F
38	H
39	K
40	G

If you score . . .

0–11	12–27	28–40
you are unlikely to get an acceptable score under examination conditions and we recommend that you spend a lot of time improving your English before you take IELTS.	you may get an acceptable score under examination conditions but we recommend that you think about having more practice or lessons before you take IELTS.	you are likely to get an acceptable score under examination conditions but remember that different institutions will find different scores acceptable.

TEST 2

LISTENING

Section 1, Questions 1–10

1	27 Bank Road
2	(a) dentist
3	Sable
4	Northern Star
5	stolen
6	Paynter
7	brother-in-law
8	(travel(ling/ing)) (to) work
9	Red Flag
10	450

Section 2, Questions 11–20

11	City Bridge
12	Newtown
13	6.30
14	(formal) garden
15	(Tower) Restaurant
16	view(s)
17	history
18	7 screen
19	every 20 minutes
20	(from/the) Central Station

Section 3, Questions 21–30

21	B
22	A
23	C
24	B
25	A
26	B
27	1882 (to/-) (18)83
28	signed
29&30	*IN EITHER ORDER*
	A
	D

Section 4, Questions 31–40

31	C
32	B
33	C
34	A
35	A
36	2 directions
37	confident
38	vision
39	corrections
40	balance

If you score . . .

0–11	12–27	28–40
you are unlikely to get an acceptable score under examination conditions and we recommend that you spend a lot of time improving your English before you take IELTS.	you may get an acceptable score under examination conditions but we recommend that you think about having more practice or lessons before you take IELTS.	you are likely to get an acceptable score under examination conditions but remember that different institutions will find different scores acceptable.

ACADEMIC READING

Reading Passage 1, Questions 1–13

1 YES
2 NO
3 NOT GIVEN
4 YES
5 B
6 A
7 B
8 C
9 A
10 C
11 D
12 C
13 C

Reading Passage 2, Questions 14–26

14 E
15 B
16 C
17 B
18 YES
19 NOT GIVEN
20 NO

21 YES
22 food bills/costs
23 (modern) intensive farming
24 organic farming
25 Greener Food Standard
26 ***IN EITHER ORDER***
    farmers (and)
    consumers

Reading Passage 3, Questions 27–40

27 ii
28 v
29 x
30 i
31 NO
32 YES
33 NO
34 YES
35 NOT GIVEN
36 D
37 I
38 G
39 E
40 B

If you score . . .

0–13	14–29	30–40
you are unlikely to get an acceptable score under examination conditions and we recommend that you spend a lot of time improving your English before you take IELTS.	you may get an acceptable score under examination conditions but we recommend that you think about having more practice or lessons before you take IELTS.	you are likely to get an acceptable score under examination conditions but remember that different institutions will find different scores acceptable.

TEST 3

LISTENING

Section 1, Questions 1–10

1   business
2   third
3   Sport(s) Centre
4   (a) cleaner
5   Library
6   International House
7   B659
8   (an) office assistant
9   answer (the) phone
10 11.30

Section 2 , Questions 11–20

11 B
12 C
13 A
14 C' ✗
15 B
16 A
17 forest
18 temple
19 waterfall
20 village↲

Section 3, Questions 21–30

21 cigar
22 13 (different) countries
23 activated ↙
24 50 km(s)
25 temperature
26 A
27 C
28 A
29 B
30 C

Section 4, Questions 31–40

31 B
32 B
33 A
34 C
35 business
36 kitchen
37 world
38 escape
39 baby
40 chocolate

If you score . . .

0–11	12–27	28–40
you are unlikely to get an acceptable score under examination conditions and we recommend that you spend a lot of time improving your English before you take IELTS.	you may get an acceptable score under examination conditions but we recommend that you think about having more practice or lessons before you take IELTS.	you are likely to get an acceptable score under examination conditions but remember that different institutions will find different scores acceptable.

ACADEMIC READING

Reading Passage 1, Questions 1–13

1	FALSE
2	TRUE
3	NOT GIVEN
4	TRUE
5	FALSE
6	NOT GIVEN
7	C
8	M
9	F
10	D
11	N
12	O
13	E

Reading Passage 2, Questions 14–26

14	iv
15	vii
16	x
17	i
18	vi
19	ii
20	E
21	D
22	C
23	B
24	A
25	A
26	A

Reading Passage 3, Questions 27–40

27	NOT GIVEN
28	FALSE
29	TRUE
30	FALSE
31	FALSE
32	FALSE
33	TRUE
34	J
35	A
36	E
37	B
38	G
39	D
40	B

If you score . . .

0–13	14–30	31–40
you are unlikely to get an acceptable score under examination conditions and we recommend that you spend a lot of time improving your English before you take IELTS.	you may get an acceptable score under examination conditions but we recommend that you think about having more practice or lessons before you take IELTS.	you are likely to get an acceptable score under examination conditions but remember that different institutions will find different scores acceptable.

TEST 4

LISTENING

Section 1, Questions 1–10

1	Keiko
2	JO6337
3	4 months
4	(Advanced) English (Studies)
5	(young) children
6	pets
7	seafood
8	tennis
9	trains/(the) train
10	this/that afternoon

Section 2, Questions 11–20

11	C
12	B
13	A
14	B
15	car park
16	rose garden
17	café
18	cycling
19	biology lesson
20	viewing shelter

Section 3, Questions 21–30

21	5
22	assessed
23	A
24	B
25	A
26	C
27	media room
28	resources room
29	embassy
30	statistics/stats

Section 4, Questions 31–40

31	B
32	C
33	A
34	water
35&36	***IN EITHER ORDER***
	meat
	cheese
37	5th/new taste
38	common
39	bitterness
40	minerals

If you score . . .

0–11	12–27	28–40
you are unlikely to get an acceptable score under examination conditions and we recommend that you spend a lot of time improving your English before you take IELTS.	you may get an acceptable score under examination conditions but we recommend that you think about having more practice or lessons before you take IELTS.	you are likely to get an acceptable score under examination conditions but remember that different institutions will find different scores acceptable.

ACADEMIC READING

Reading Passage 1, Questions 1–13

1	TRUE
2	FALSE
3	NOT GIVEN
4	TRUE
5	FALSE
6	NOT GIVEN
7	TRUE
8	(wooden) pulleys
9	stone
10	(accomplished) sailors
11	(modern) glider
12	flight
13	messages

Reading Passage 2, Questions 14–26

14	FALSE
15	NOT GIVEN
16	TRUE
17	NOT GIVEN
18	TRUE
19	TRUE
20	FALSE
21	G
22	E
23	B
24	A
25	K
26	F

Reading Passage 3, Questions 27–40

27	D
28	C
29	A
30	B
31	D
32	F
33	I
34	B
35	A
36	D
37	A
38	E
39	B
40	C

If you score . . .

0–11	12–27	28–40
you are unlikely to get an acceptable score under examination conditions and we recommend that you spend a lot of time improving your English before you take IELTS.	you may get an acceptable score under examination conditions but we recommend that you think about having more practice or lessons before you take IELTS.	you are likely to get an acceptable score under examination conditions but remember that different institutions will find different scores acceptable.

GENERAL TRAINING TEST A

Section 1, Questions 1–14

1 FALSE
2 TRUE
3 NOT GIVEN
4 TRUE
5 FALSE
6 FALSE
7 TRUE
8 v
9 vii
10 ix
11 ii
12 x
13 i
14 iii

Section 2, Questions 15–27

15 image
16 passing trade
17 access
18 walls
19 contract
20 housing
21 their department
22 (the) supervisor
23 exempt employees
24 Human Resources/HR
25 (a) prorated system
26 Leave Request forms
27 (a) grace period

Section 3, Questions 28–40

28 B
29 D
30 B
31 C
32 C
33–36 *IN ANY ORDER*
    D
    E
    F
    I
37 FALSE
38 TRUE
39 NOT GIVEN
40 FALSE

If you score . . .

0–15	16–27	28–40
you are unlikely to get an acceptable score under examination conditions and we recommend that you spend a lot of time improving your English before you take IELTS.	you may get an acceptable score under examination conditions but we recommend that you think about having more practice or lessons before you take IELTS.	you are likely to get an acceptable score under examination conditions but remember that different institutions will find different scores acceptable.

GENERAL TRAINING TEST B

Section 1, Questions 1–14

1 C
2 D
3 A
4 B
5 C
6 D
7 A
8 FALSE
9 TRUE
10 NOT GIVEN
11 NOT GIVEN
12 FALSE
13 TRUE
14 TRUE

Section 2, Questions 15–27

15 family business
16 training
17 accommodation
18 (the) payroll
19 employer(s)
20 pay records
21 3/three months
22 (obvious) spam
23 message time
24 prompt attention
25 reply immediately
26 brief acknowledgement
27 (definite) date

Section 3, Questions 28–40

28 1638
29 1781
30 1934
31 2001
32 TRUE
33 FALSE
34 FALSE
35 NOT GIVEN
36 TRUE
37 D
38 E
39 C
40 H

If you score . . .

0–17	18–29	30–40
you are unlikely to get an acceptable score under examination conditions and we recommend that you spend a lot of time improving your English before you take IELTS.	you may get an acceptable score under examination conditions but we recommend that you think about having more practice or lessons before you take IELTS.	you are likely to get an acceptable score under examination conditions but remember that different institutions will find different scores acceptable.

Model and sample answers for Writing tasks

TEST 1, WRITING TASK 1

SAMPLE ANSWER

This is an answer written by a candidate who achieved a **Band 5.5** score. Here is the examiner's comment:

> This answer focuses on the key features of the information, clearly grouping the countries, using supporting figures and presenting an overview. However, there is no clear reference to what the percentages represent and key comparisons need more expansion.
>
> Information is organised with clear signalling and some effective referencing and linking, although not all ideas are clearly linked and the overall progression is achieved by repetition in the final section.
>
> The range of vocabulary is rather narrow and just sufficient for the task. The attempt to paraphrase the rubric shows limited flexibility. There are several spelling and word form errors, and quite a lot of repetition. Similarly, the range of sentence forms is not wide, with few examples of complex structures. However, apart from one or two errors in basic grammar, simple structures are accurate and easily understood.

Different countries' consumer spendings are quite different. The table shows the vary consumer spending on a seires of intems in the five countries, namely, the Ireland, Italy, Span, Sweden and Turkey in 2002.

Food, drinks and tobacco were in the most important position on consumer spending in all of the five countries, and in a different percentage. In Ireland and turkey. they were near 30%, while in the other three countries they are under 20%.

Clothing and footwear were the second important consumer spending in these countries. In Italy, they got 9%, and in Sweden, they were 5.4%. In the other three countries, the figure were very similar, all were near 6.5%.

The last consumer spending were leisure and education. In Turkey, they were 4.35%, and in the other four countries the figure were under 4%.

In conclusion, it can be said that in 2002, food, drinks and tabacoo were the most important consumer spending in the five countries, and the different countries' consumer spending were quite different.

TEST 1, WRITING TASK 2

MODEL ANSWER

This model has been prepared by an examiner as an example of a very good answer. However, please note that this is just one example out of many possible approaches.

The relative importance of natural talent and training is a frequent topic of discussion when people try to explain different levels of ability in, for example, sport, art or music.

Obviously, education systems are based on the belief that all children can effectively be taught to acquire different skills, including those associated with sport, art or music. So from our own school experience, we can find plenty of evidence to support the view that a child can acquire these skills with continued teaching and guided practice.

However, some people believe that innate talent is what differentiates a person who has been trained to play a sport or an instrument, from those who become good players. In other words, there is more to the skill than a learned technique, and this extra talent cannot be taught, no matter how good the teacher or how frequently a child practices.

I personally think that some people do have talents that are probably inherited via their genes. Such talents can give individuals a facility for certain skills that allow them to excel, while more hard-working students never manage to reach a comparable level. But, as with all questions of nature versus nurture, they are not mutually exclusive. Good musicians or artists and exceptional sports stars have probably succeeded because of both good training and natural talent. Without the natural talent, continuous training would be neither attractive nor productive, and without the training, the child would not learn how to exploit and develop their talent.

In conclusion, I agree that any child can be taught particular skills, but to be really good in areas such as music, art or sport, then some natural talent is required.

TEST 2, WRITING TASK 1

MODEL ANSWER

This model has been prepared by an examiner as an example of a very good answer. However, please note that this is just one example out of many possible approaches.

The graph illustrates changes in the amounts of beef, lamb, chicken and fish consumed in a particular European country between 1979 and 2004.

In 1979 beef was by far the most popular of these foods, with about 225 grams consumed per person per week. Lamb and chicken were eaten in similar quantities (around 150 grams), while much less fish was consumed (just over 50 grams).

However, during this 25-year period the consumption of beef and lamb fell dramatically to approximately 100 grams and 55 grams respectively. The consumption of fish also declined, but much less significantly to just below 50 grams, so although it remained the least popular food, consumption levels were the most stable.

The consumption of chicken, on the other hand, showed an upward trend, overtaking that of lamb in 1980 and that of beef in 1989. By 2004 it had soared to almost 250 grams per person per week.

Overall, the graph shows how the consumption of chicken increased dramatically while the popularity of these other foods decreased over the period.